THE NATURE OF THE SELF

The Nature of the Self

A FUNCTIONAL INTERPRETATION

by Risieri Frondizi

NEW HAVEN: YALE UNIVERSITY PRESS, 1953

London: Geoffrey Cumberlege, Oxford University Press

Preface

The concept of substance as a simple, immutable, independent entity seems to be inadequate today as the basic category in the interpretation of reality. Science and philosophy in the last 200 years, in their effort to understand physical and human facts, have not only accumulated weighty proofs demonstrating the limitations of the substantialist conception but have suggested the categories which must be substituted for that idea. Better adapted to the explanation of reality in general and mind in particular are the more recent concepts of function, process, relation, activity, and *Gestalt*.

It is no less true, to be sure, that in its time the substantialist thesis filled a very real need. It gave unity to the world picture of its era, and its influence has been so great that it is found even today in the form of assumptions and presuppositions embedded in doctrines which claim to be antisubstantialist. The substantialist assumptions of such doctrines can be detected if we pay more attention to the way the problems are presented to us than to their solutions. It is unnecessary, of course, to insist upon the great significance of the way a problem is put in the development of philosophic doctrine.

If one wishes to avoid deceptive ways of stating the problems one must first of all examine the interweaving of presuppositions and interests which lies behind the different philosophic doctrines. The present study is directed toward this end, particularly with regard to the problem of the self.

The development of an adequate theory of the self has been obstructed by a fallacious dilemma which attempts to force us to choose between a substantial self and no self at all. In other words, according to this dilemma, only two paths are open to us: either we postulate a metaphysical entity which assures us of the continuity of the self, ignoring its ever-changing nature, or we emphasize the empirical data which affirm the flux of the self but which cannot explain its unity and continuity. Whichever we choose of the two extremes, our doctrine will be vitiated by a narrow attitude which does not conceive of any existence other than substantial.

Historically, Descartes and Hume represent the two extremes of the dilemma which is still blocking the way to a fruitful approach to the nature of the self in spite of attempts already made. Only a close examination of the significance and development of both positions—historically united as they are by the slow process of the dissolution of the first until it ended in the second—will permit us to rid ourselves of deceptive ways of looking at the problem without renouncing the experience and the valid contributions of those who have previously studied the question.

Once the ground is cleared of the limitations of an attitude based on an unfounded assumption, I intend in the second part of this study to extract from experience itself the concepts which explain the continuity and unity of the self without neglecting its changing nature, for neither characteristic is more real than the other.

As to the value of the concepts of function and Gestalt as substitutes for the category of substance—which converted the self into an immutable, simple, and independent entity—the reader will be able to judge for himself after having read this work. It is requested only that in reading these pages he shall not interpret words in his own sense or even in their accustomed meaning but rather in the sense in which they are used in the text and which a careful reading, it is hoped, will unequivocally reveal. The understanding of a philosophical work requires the capacity to rid oneself, at least temporarily, of the *idola fori* which inhabit the mind.

It is, finally, necessary to keep in mind that we are dealing here with the self from the psychological point of view and that all the problems of the relationship of the Ego to the other selves, the body, and the world in general have been deliberately put aside for later analysis.

My grateful thanks are due to Elias L. Rivers who translated several parts of the book from Spanish into English, to Miss C. Virginia Matters for suggesting many improvements in expression, and to Professor Adolfo P. Carpio who kindly read the galley proofs. I owe a special debt to Professors Brand Blanshard, E. S. Brightman, and Paul Weiss, who read and criticized the entire manuscript. Acknowledgment is also due to the University of

Puerto Rico and the Bollingen Foundation for their generous grants and to the Yale University Press for its interest in the publication of the book. From start to finish I received the constant help and encouragement of my wife, to whom I wish to express my thanks once more.

I want to acknowledge with thanks the courtesy of the publishers of the following books from which quotations have been made:

K. Koffka, *Principles of Gestalt Psychology* (New York, Harcourt, Brace & Co., 1935); C. W. Morris, *Six Theories of Mind* (The University of Chicago Press, 1932); D. H. Parker, *Experience and Substance* (The University of Michigan Press, 1941); *The Works of George Berkeley*, ed. by A. C. Fraser, 4 vols. (Oxford, Clarendon Press, 1901).

R. F.

University of Puerto Rico
Río Piedras, Puerto Rico
December 30, 1952

Contents

ix

Part I

ORIGIN AND DISSOLUTION OF THE MODERN DOCTRINE OF THE SELF AS SUBSTANCE

CHAPTER I

Descartes and the Thinking Substance

1. From cogito to res cogitans

The modern conception of the self begins with Descartes's discovery of the *cogito*. It was really something new, despite an external similarity to the doctrines of St. Augustine and Campanella, for the cogito in Descartes acquired a meaning that it had not had before. And it was Descartes who set modern thought upon a course heretofore untraveled.[1]

1. During his own lifetime Descartes heard the objection that due to the Augustinian precedent there was nothing new in his doctrine of the cogito. Mersenne was the first, after reading the *Discourse on Method*, to call Descartes's attention to the similarity of his argument and that of St. Augustine in the *De Civitate Dei*, 11, 26. Descartes answered, "il ne me semble pas s'en servir à même usage que je fais." Letter to Mersenne, May 25, 1637, ed. Adam-Tannery, 1, 376.

Arnauld emphasizes this point in his objections to the *Meditations*, indicating the similarity of Descartes's attitude and St. Augustine's in the *De Libero Arbitrio*, 2, 3 n. 7, and in a passage of the *De Trinitate*, 10, 10 n. 12. Letter dated June 3, 1648, ed. Adam-Tannery, 5, 186.

Recently L. Blanchet and É. Gilson have thoroughly studied

Today it seems impossible to return to the old type of realism, and modern philosophy—even that branch of it called realist—shows the indelible mark of Descartes.[2] But Descartes could not free himself completely from the realism of the past, and his discovery of the cogito was limited by a series of prejudices which he owed to his scholastic training and from which he could not entirely free his thought. These prejudices acted in the guise of presuppositions and from the very beginning limited not only his initial discovery but also the whole development of the Cartesian system—and, in particular, his conception of the self.

Descartes begins his meditations with the immediate purpose of establishing a primary truth, "certain and indubitable," that would not only serve him as a secure point of departure but would also allow him to extract the

---

the antecedents of the cogito in works that have already become known as authoritative: Léon Blanchet, *Les Antécedents historiques du "je pense, donc je suis"* (Paris, Alcan, 1920); and Étienne Gilson, *Études sur le rôle de la pensée médiévale dans la formation du système cartésien* (Paris, J. Vrin, 1930). Besides making a study of the Augustinian antecedents, in the second part of his work Blanchet studies Campanella's conception as a forerunner of Descartes's. Of especial interest with respect to our work is chap. iv of the second part, on "la certitude de la consciénce de soi" in the Calabrian philosopher. In Gilson's work, see chap. ii of the second part and chap. i of the appendix.

Cf. also A. Koyré, *Descartes und die Scholastik* (Bonn, 1923).

2. Whitehead is correct when he writes that "philosophy never reverts to its old position after the shock of a great philosopher." *Process and Reality* (New York, Macmillan, 1941), p. 16.

criterion of truth itself.[3] His secondary purpose was "faire connaître que ce moi qui pense est une substance immatérielle,"[4] as he himself expresses it in a letter dated November 1640.

The thesis that the self is an immaterial substance contains all the greatness and limitations of the Cartesian conception. On the one hand, this conception illustrates a substantial reality that can be seen from within, the self being the only substance that can give us a view of its inner nature. Descartes believes that he has directly and immediately made evident, without conceptual evasions and complications, the existence of a substance as something that needs only itself in order to exist. At the same time he sets substantialism on the new and fertile path of modern idealism. In this lies the greatness of the Cartesian conception, but it carries within itself a serious limitation— the discovery of the cogito is weighed down, in all its derivations and consequences, by the category of substance, which is a very heavy load.

The procedure that Descartes uses to arrive at the cogito is well known. He begins by doubting everything and discovers that there is something he cannot doubt, which is, of course, the very fact that he is doubting. And as long as he doubts—or thinks—he exists. In other words, doubt can eat away at the content of consciousness —I can doubt the existence of things that I see or imagine

3. Cf. *Discourse on Method*, Pt. IV, and *Metaphysical Meditations*, Third Meditation.

4. Cf. *Oeuvres de Descartes*, ed. Adam-Tannery (Paris, 1897–1909), 3, 247.

—but it cannot reach the experience of doubt iself. This is the famous *cogito ergo sum.*

This primary truth is immediately vitiated, to some extent at least, by the clandestine introduction of a thesis that has not undergone the severe proof to which Descartes was determined to submit every idea or principle. As a matter of fact, once sure of his own existence, Descartes turns his attention to the nature of his existence. He writes in the *Metaphysical Meditations:* "But I do not yet know clearly enough what I am, I who am certain that I am." [5] After examining various possibilities critically and rejecting them, he reaches the conclusion that "I find here that thought is an attribute that belongs to me; it alone cannot be separated from me." [6]

Up to this point his line of reasoning seems completely logical. There is a concealed prejudice, however, in the form of a presupposition, and it comes up as a pat linguistic formula rather than as a concept or a theory.[7] Descartes goes on, as a matter of fact, by saying, "I do not now admit anything which is not necessarily true: to speak accurately I am not more than a thing which thinks . . . I am, however, a real thing and really exist; but what thing? I have answered: a thing which thinks." [8]

5. *Meditations,* II (*The Philosophical Works of Descartes,* tr. E. Haldane and G. Ross [Cambridge, 1931], 1, 150).

6. *Ibid.* (1, 151).

7. Especially in the *Discourse on Method,* as we shall soon see.

8. *Meditations,* II (1, 152). The complete text of the Latin original runs as follows: "Nihil nunc admitto nisi quod necessario sit verum; sum igitur praecise tantum res cogitans, id est, mens,

His line of reasoning in the *Discourse on Method*, although set forth in a more synthetic form, is similar to that seen in the *Meditations*. A study of the way he moves from the cogito to the *res cogitans* in the *Discourse* will be of interest inasmuch as this is the earliest work in which he sets forth this transition. There is also the fact that the French language, in which this work was originally written, allows one to play with words—especially with the term *chose*—with more facility than in Latin. Here is the central passage:

> But immediately afterwards I noticed that whilst I thus wished to think all things false, it was absolutely essential that the "I" who thought this should be something, and remarking that this truth *"I think, therefore I am"* was so certain and so assured that all the most extravagant suppositions brought forward by the sceptics were incapable of shaking it, I came to the conclusion that I could receive it without scruple as the first principle of the Philosophy for which I was seeking.
>
> And then, examining attentively that which I was, I saw that I could conceive that I had no body, and that there was no world nor place where I might be; but yet that I could not for all that conceive that I

sive animus, sive intellectus, sive ratio, voces mihi prius significationis ignotae. Sum autem res vera, & vere existens; sed qualis res? Dixi, cogitans." Ed. Adam-Tannery, 7, 27.

(The original text will be provided in footnotes whenever it is possible that the translation may have distorted its meaning or may give rise to doubts as to the interpretation proposed.)

was not. On the contrary, I saw from the very fact that I thought of doubting the truth of other things, it very evidently and certainly followed that I was; on the other hand if I had only ceased from thinking, even if all the rest of what I had ever imagined had really existed, I should have no reason for thinking that I had existed. From that I knew that I was a substance the whole essence or nature of which is to think . . .[9]

9. *Discourse on Method*, tr. Haldane-Ross, p. 101.
The complete text in the original French runs as follows: "Mais, aussitôt après, je pris garde que, pendant que je voulais ainsi penser que tout était faux, il fallait nécessairement que moi, qui le pensais, fusse quelque chose. Et remarquant que cette vérité: *je pense, donc je suis*, était si ferme et si assurée, que toutes les plus extravagantes suppositions des sceptiques n'étaient pas capables de l'ébranler, je jugeai que je pouvais la recevoir, sans scrupule, pour le premier principe de la philosophie, que je cherchais.

"Puis, examinant avec attention ce que j'étais, et voyant que je pouvais feindre que je n'avais aucun corps, et qu'il n'y avait aucun monde, ni aucun lieu où je fusse; mais que je ne ne pouvais feindre, pour cela, que je n'étais point; et qu'au contraire, de cela même que je pensais à douter de la vérité des autres choses, il suivait très évidemment et très certainement que j'étais; au lieu que, si j'eusse seulement cessé de penser, encore que tout le reste de ce que j'avais jamais imaginé eût été vrai, je n'avais aucune raison de croire que j'eusse été: je connus de là que j'étais une substance dont tout l'essence ou la nature n'est que de penser, et qui, pour être, n'a besoin d'aucun lieu, ni ne dépend d'aucune chose matérielle." Ed. É. Gilson (Paris, J. Vrin, 1930), pp. 32-3.

As can be seen, Descartes—in both the *Discourse on Method* and the *Metaphysical Meditations*—moves from the naïve expression "something" (*quelque chose*), which implies no philosophical presuppositions, to the affirmation of the "thinking thing" as a substance. The psychologico-linguistic process by which he falls back on the substantialist thesis is as follows: "If I exist, I must be some *thing* [in the sense of 'something']. But what thing? A thing [*res*] that thinks." In this process the word "thing," which at first lacks philosophical import, clandestinely acquires a theoretical meaning, but no new idea has been introduced to justify this transformation.

2. *The substantialist presupposition*

This is the line of reasoning followed by Descartes, according to his basic writings. It does seem to be rather naïve to believe, however—as some of the logical positivists today maintain—that the movement from the cogito to the res cogitans is no more than a bit of linguistic sleight of hand that has metaphysical consequences. As a matter of fact, it is just the reverse. This is not a metaphysical position that originates in a linguistic habit but rather a linguistic usage that derives from a metaphysical doctrine.

If Descartes had been completely consistent in following the consequences of his first attitude and had not allowed himself to be influenced by substantialist prejudices, the jump from the cogito to the *substantia cogitans* would not have been made, and the whole history of the modern theory of the self would have been different.

What Descartes does prove by means of his doubt is the existence of a thinking activity, the cogito; all that he can legitimately infer from this is the *sum* of this activity. However, he not only affirms the existence of a subject that thinks and exists but also states, without any elaboration, that its nature is substantial. Why does Descartes avoid the problem of the existence of the self?[1] Why does he abandon, at the very beginning of the constructive phase of his reasoning, the rigorous and cautious attitude with which he had begun and thus pass lightly over such fundamental problems? It must be because he is imbued with a substantialist outlook, not only as a doctrine but also in the form of prejudices or presuppositions.[2] This presupposition keeps him from seeing the problem of the existence of the self, for he assumes that the activity of thinking could not exist without a thinking subject. Thus it is that at the very moment in which he reaches the cogito he sets up in opposition to it the thinking subject, as we have seen in the passage quoted above from the *Discourse on Method:* "But immediately afterwards I noticed that whilst I thus wished to think all

1. That the existence of a cogito without an Ego is a possibility and a real problem is evident from the later position of Hume which has continued to hold sway until our own day in thinkers of the high caliber of William James and Bertrand Russell.

2. What I mean by the substantialist prejudice is the presupposition that the existence of a phenomenon, activity, quality, etc., presupposes the existence of a substance as a substratum that supports it. This prejudice brings with it the implicit presupposition that there can be no activity without subject, no thought —in the Cartesian sense—without a thinking self.

things false, it was absolutely essential that the 'I' who thought this should be something . . ."

The importance of the substantialist presupposition is made quite obvious if one observes Descartes's attitude before and after he arrives at the cogito. Before his discovery of the cogito, he lays hands on every possible recourse, including the famous hypothesis of the *malin génie*, in order to increase his critical capacity with regard to supposed truths. After the cogito, not only does he fail to doubt very dubious things but he permits complete metaphysical doctrines to slip in furtively, with all their trappings and consequences.

This prejudice not only functions as a steppingstone with which he steps over many problems in the transition from the cogito to the res cogitans but also becomes one of the principal postulates of his whole theory. He writes in the *Principles of Philosophy* (1, para. 11) that "it is very manifest by the natural light which is in our souls, that no qualities or properties pertain to nothing; [3] and that where some are perceived there must necessarily be some thing or substance on which they depend." [4] He restates this attitude farther on (1, para. 52) when he

3. Descartes said the same thing some time before (1641) in the fifth definition that follows the replies to the second objections: "For by means of our natural light we know that a real attribute cannot be an attribute of nothing." Ed. Haldane-Ross, 2, 53. The Latin text: "quia naturali lumine notum est, nullum esse posse nihili reale attributum." Ed. Adam-Tannery, 7, 161.

4. The Latin original reads as follows: "notandum est, lumine naturali esse notissimum, nihili nullas esse affectiones sive qualitates; atque ideo ubicumque aliquas deprehendimus, ibi rem sive

writes that "it is a common notion that nothing is possessed of no attributes, properties, or qualities. For this reason, when we perceive any attribute, we therefore conclude that some existing thing or substance to which it may be attributed, is necessarily present." [5]

3. Mind as thinking substance

This is how, in my opinion, Descartes arrives at the conception of the self as thinking substance. In order to make his theory clear it is necessary to study, at least briefly, his conception of substance. Descartes defines substance as "a thing which so exists that it needs no other thing in order to exist." [6] He observes that if one takes this definition in the strictest sense there would be only a single substance, God, for "all other things can exist only by the help of the concourse of God." [7]

This would prove that the concept of substance is not univocal. But the equivocation may be avoided by making a distinction between God and the created substances. In the future when we speak of substances we will be refer-

---

substantiam, cujus illae sint, necessario inveniri . . ." Ed. Adam-Tannery, 8, 8.

5. "quod nihili nulla sint attributa, nullaeve proprietates aut qualitates. Ex hoc enim quod aliquod attributum adesse percipiamus, concludimus aliquam rem existentem, sive substantiam, cui illud tribui possit, necessario etiam adesse." Ed. Adam-Tannery, 8, 25.

6. *Princ. Phil.*, 1, para. 51. "Per *substantiam* nihil aliud intelligere possumus, quam rem quae ita existit, ut nulla alia re indigeat ad existendum." Ed. Adam-Tannery, 8, 24.

7. *Ibid.*

ing to the latter, which are all that interest us here. As was the custom, Descartes distinguishes these substances from their qualities or attributes.

The notion of substance, in this latter sense, is applied to immaterial things as well as to those that are corporeal; the only condition is that they be able to exist without the aid of any other created thing. This conception of substance as something that does not need anything other than itself in order to exist leads Descartes to maintain the mutual exclusion of substances, with all the consequences that such a doctrine implies. Although this notion of substance seems clear enough on the surface, the knowledge that we have of substances is not easily attainable, for, as Descartes recognizes, we do not perceive their existence directly but rather through their observable attributes.[8]

How can we be sure of the existence of substance if we can only observe its attributes? Descartes's reply is quite clear. Nothingness does not have attributes, and therefore from the presence of an attribute we can with certainty infer the existence of a substance that supports it.[9] It is from this point of view that he characterizes substance in the definitions that he adds to the replies to the second objections. He writes, "Everything in which there resides immediately, as in a subject, or by means of which there exists anything that we perceive, i.e., any property, quality,

8. *Princ. Phil.*, 1, para. 52. In his reply to Hobbes' objection to the second meditation Descartes writes that "we do not know substance immediately and in itself, but in that it is the subject of certain acts." Cf. ed. Adam-Tannery, 9, 136.

9. See above, p. 11 nn. 3, 4, p. 12 n. 5.

or attribute, of which we have a real idea, is called a *Substance*." [1]

If the knowledge that we have of the existence of substance is the result of an inference, based in turn upon a presupposition, we should be surer concerning the datum that allows us to carry out the inference than concerning the conclusion of the inference itself. That is, the presence of the attribute should be more certain than the presence of substance. But Descartes does not seem to think so. After jumping from the attribute to the substance, he conceives of the latter as intimately joined to the former and states that we have a clear and distinct idea of substance along with its concomitant attribute.[2] If we insist upon knowing what substance is when its attributes have been removed, Descartes will reply that substance always occurs along with its attributes and that the two cannot be separated. It is true, though, that substance and attribute are not one and the same thing for Descartes, and it is therefore legitimate to want to know what substance is when deprived of its attributes. It appears that it is impossible to apply to the general concept of substance Descartes's own definition—that it is something that needs nothing besides itself in order to exist —for substance cannot exist by itself. It must necessarily be either thinking substance or extended substance; that is, it cannot exist without the attribute which belongs to it.

The English analytical spirit broke down the unity of

1. Ed. Haldane-Ross, 2, 53.
2. Cf. *Princ. Phil.*, 1, para. 54.

substance by distinguishing it sharply from its attributes and by studying them both according to empirical criteria. If it is true, as Descartes believed, that substance cannot exist in separation from its attribute and if the attribute is the only aspect that we can know empirically, substance is transformed—as actually happened in the cases of Locke and Berkeley—into an empty and unknowable support for its qualities.

It is unquestionable that in Cartesian thought the connection between substance and its attributes is so intimate that not only is it impossible for an attribute to exist without belonging to a substance or for a substance to exist without its attributes but every substance has a principal attribute or basic property "which constitutes its nature and essence." [3] As we know, extension is the principal attribute of material substance, and thought is that of thinking substance. Everything else that can be attributed to a body presupposes extension; we cannot conceive of shape or movement without extension, while we can conceive of extension without shape and movement. In the same way, whatever we find in the mind is a mode of thought so that one cannot conceive of imagination, sentiment, or will, for example, without thought, while one can conceive of thought without imagination or sentiment.[4]

The intimate connection between attribute and substance leads Descartes to affirm that the soul is always

3. *Ibid.*, 1, para. 53. Ed. Haldane-Ross, 1, 240.

4. For the distinction between "mode," "quality," and "attribute," see *Princ. Phil.*, 1, para. 56.

thinking. In fact, if it ceased to think it would cease to be, for its existence depends on its essential attribute. For Descartes this is an a priori matter. But empiricism did not understand it in this fashion, and thus Locke denies that the soul is always thinking.[5]

By "thought" Descartes does not mean what is usually designated by this term at the present time. In the second meditation he makes it clear that a thing which thinks "is a thing which doubts, understands, conceives, affirms, denies, wills, refuses, which also imagines and feels." [6] In the *Principles of Philosophy* he writes, similarly, that "by the word thought (*cogitatio*) I understand all that of which we are conscious as operating in us." [7]

Such, in brief, is the meaning of the Cartesian conception of the soul as a thinking substance, which, as we shall see in the following chapter, is broken down by Locke's analytic treatment and finally gives rise, after additional battering at the hands of Berkeley, to the antithetic position expressed by Hume in the *Treatise of Human Nature*.

There is no doubt at all that Descartes is the first modern philosopher to conceive of the mind as substance. This statement may perhaps be widened considerably; he is probably the first man in all the history of philosophy

5. Cf. John Locke, *Essay Concerning Human Understanding,* Bk. II, chap. i, para. 10.

6. *Meditations,* ed. Haldane-Ross, 1, 153.

7. *Princ. Phil.*, 1, para. 9 (ed. Haldane-Ross, 1, 222).

Cf. also definition I added to the replies to the second objections. Ed. Haldane-Ross, 2, 52.

to have such a conception of the mind. As we all know, scholastic philosophers considered the soul and the body as substances that are incomplete in themselves and mutually dependent; the timid attempts at substantializing either one of them never made much headway. Descartes, on the other hand, maintained as one of the cardinal principles of his philosophy "thought's" independence of "extension"; this enabled him to conceive of the mind as a true substance, that is, as something that needs nothing besides itself in order to exist. Étienne Gilson, one of the greatest scholars of medieval philosophy, who has traced in detail the antecedents of Cartesian thought, is right in maintaining that "la substantialité complète de l'âme [était] établie pour la première fois par les *Méditations métaphysiques* . . ." [8]

Whatever may have been Descartes's relation with the past, no one can doubt his influence upon later thought. Subsequent philosophy either has, in essence, drawn upon Cartesian material or has taken the system of the French thinker as its central axis of reference. In this double sense Descartes must of necessity be the point of departure for any study of the modern conception of the self.

8. Cf. his edition of Descartes's *Discours de la méthode* (Paris, J. Vrin, 1930), p. 437.

CHAPTER II

Substance as an "I-Know-not-What" and the Problem of Personal Identity in Locke

1. Cartesian origin of Locke's conception of substance

Descartes dedicated his meditations to the service of the substantialist concept which he had absorbed from his medieval sources. With his discovery of the cogito, however, he dealt substantialism a serious blow, which caused its slow but inevitable decline despite its subsequent apogee in European rationalism.

The destruction of the Cartesian concept of substance, and in particular of the thinking substance, was initiated and completed in the British Isles during the period that extends from Locke to Hume. We shall carefully look into this transformation of philosophical ideas because it will lead us to the opposite extreme of the false dilemma which I stated in the preface and which continues to obstruct the full development of a theory of the self that will do justice both to its changing nature and to its unity and continuity.

The dissolution process of the Cartesian concept of a

thinking substance begins with Locke. This does not mean that Locke sets himself up in radical opposition to Descartes—as some European handbooks of the history of philosophy erroneously maintain—but that he imposes upon the Cartesian ideas a movement which is alien to them and which initiates the rapid decline of the concept of the res cogitans.

The debt owed to Descartes by Locke is greater than is generally admitted. Locke explicitly acknowledges this debt—however greatly he may stress the discrepancies rather than the affinities between their philosophies.[1] It is easy to prove this by comparing certain passages in the *Essay Concerning Human Understanding* with the writings of the French thinker. Perhaps the reason for the scant attention paid to the affinities that exist between these two philosophers is the tendency, encouraged by the great German historians of philosophy, to contrast British empiricism with Continental rationalism and then to explain the Kantian system as a synthesis of the two movements. In the case of Locke this supposed contrast or opposition is further due to the fact that more attention has been paid to the first two books of the *Essay* than to the last two, where the affinity is more evident. Attention has been focused, moreover, exclusively upon the

1. Cf. his "First Letter to Stillingfleet," *The Works of John Locke*, 10th ed. (London, 1801), 4, 48–9. According to those who knew him well, Locke recognized that Descartes had inspired his interest in philosophy and had freed him from scholastic methods in the investigation of philosophic problems. Cf. Lady Masham's letter to Leclerc, dated Jan. 12, 1705, cited by Fox Bourne in his classic *Life of John Locke* (1876), 1, 61–2.

conclusions; the important fact that both conceptions are rooted in the same philosophical preoccupation has passed unnoticed. Why should we insist so much upon the fact that Locke rejects the doctrine of innate ideas [2] and forget that the existence of the whole first book of the *Essay* would be inexplicable but for Descartes? And this is not the only instance in which Descartes arouses Locke's interest in a problem. One could state without fear of exaggeration—a very conscientious student of the problem does admit this [3]—that without the influence of Descartes the *Essay*, as we know it, could never have been written. The central concept of Locke's work, that ideas are the adequate objects of knowledge, is of Cartesian origin.

Sometimes his debt includes more than the way of putting the problems. There are also Cartesian solutions. Restricting ourselves to matters pertinent to this study, we can see this debt right from the beginning. Locke follows Descartes almost word for word in his affirmation of the certainty of our own existence, which is the primary and fundamental thesis of Cartesian philosophy. He writes in his *Essay*, "As for *our own existence*, we perceive it so plainly and so certainly, that it neither needs nor is capable of any proof. For nothing can be more evident

2. Indeed, Locke's criticism was directed against the *principles* and not the innate *ideas* and was more concerned with the teachings of the Cambridge Platonists than with Descartes.

3. James Gibson in his book on *Locke's Theory of Knowledge and Its Historical Relations* (Cambridge, Cambridge University Press, 1931), p. 207.

to us than our own existence." [4] In the following chapter he reaffirms this: "I think it is beyond question, that man has a clear idea of his own being; he knows certainly he exists." [5]

The central idea and even the words are Cartesian. If there were any doubt, it would be dispelled by a rough draft of the *Essay* supposedly written by Locke in the summer of 1671, i.e. 19 years before the publication of his great work; there his debt on this score is expressly acknowledged. He writes, "The Understanding knows undoubtdly that while it thinks reasons or imagins it is or hath existence, or that there is something that knows and understands which according to Cartes and I thinke in truth is the most certain and undoubted proposition that can be in the minde of a man." [6]

Locke follows Descartes not only in affirming the indubitability of one's own existence but also in his procedure for attaining this certainty: "If I doubt of all other things, that very doubt makes me perceive my own existence . . ." [7] Here he reproduces the very words of Descartes,[8] though admittedly the argument in Locke is more by way of illustration than proof, for, as we have seen, our

4. *Essay*, IV, ix, 3. Quotations are from the standard edition of Alexander Campbell Fraser (Oxford, 1894).

5. *Ibid.*, IV, x, 2.

6. *An Early Draft of Locke's Essay Together with Excerpts from His Journals*, ed. R. I. Aaron and J. Gibb (Oxford, Clarendon Press, 1936), p. 40.

7. *Essay*, IV, ix, 3.

8. As will be recalled, Descartes writes in the *Discourse on Method*, Pt. IV: "from the very fact that I thought of doubting

own existence "neither needs nor is capable of any proof."

And his debt does not stop here. Despite the fact that Locke is going to attack the idea of substance, the substantialist conception so appeals to him that he follows Descartes in the two false steps which have been pointed out in the previous chapter. In the passage that we have just analyzed, which is the basic text in the *Essay* concerned with the knowledge of our own existence, Locke writes, "I think, I reason, I feel pleasure and pain: can any of these be more evident to me than my own existence?" [9] The presupposition upon which this argument is based seems clear. There can be no activity without a subject, or as we should say today, no experience without a self—an axiom that Hume was destined to demolish. Locke goes right on and follows Descartes in the second step, which is the affirmation of the substantiality of the subject. "If I know I doubt, I have as certain perception of the existence of the thing doubting, as of that thought which I call doubt." [1] What is this "thing doubting" but the very "thinking thing" or res cogitans of Descartes?

---

the truth of other things, it very evidently and certainly followed that I was . . ." Tr. Haldane-Ross, p. 101.

9. *Essay*, IV, ix, 3. And further on in the same passage he adds, to confirm what he has said, that "if I know I feel pain, it is evident I have as certain perception of my own existence, as of the existence of the pain I feel."

1. *Ibid*. In another context he expresses a similar idea: "We know certainly, by experience, that we *sometimes* think; and thence draw this infallible consequence,—that there is something in us that has a power to think." II, i, 10. He then states that this "something" is a substance.

This substantialist presupposition is likewise noted in a preceding chapter devoted to a different subject, which reads: "It is past controversy, that we have in us *something* that thinks; our very doubts about what it is, confirm the certainty of its being." [2] Actually, doubt proves the existence not of a thinking subject but of the act of thinking or of doubting.

The recognition of our own existence was not for Locke —or for Descartes either—the result of a process of reasoning. "We have the knowledge of our own existence by intuition," he writes in various passages of the *Essay*.[3] And he characterizes intuition in terms similar to those of Descartes.[4] Knowledge is intuitive for Locke when the mind perceives the agreement or disagreement of two ideas immediately by themselves, without the intervention of any other. In these cases the mind perceives the truth just as the eye does light, i.e. merely by looking.[5] Naturally, intuition is the clearest and most certain form of knowledge; there is no room for doubt. And upon intuition depends the certainty and evidence of all our knowledge.[6]

Locke is in agreement with Descartes in this whole

2. *Ibid.*, IV, iii, 6.
3. Cf. *ibid.*, IV, ix, 2; IV, ix, 3; IV, xi, 1.
4. Cf. *Essay*, IV, ii. This second chapter is very similar to the beginning of Descartes's *Regulae ad Directionem Ingenii*. Though it is true that the *Rules* (1701) were published 11 years after the *Essay* (1690), we know that many manuscript copies were circulated prior to publication, and it is probable that Locke used one of these copies while he was in France.
5. Cf. *Essay*, IV, ii, 1.
6. *Ibid.*

argument concerning the certainty of one's own existence, but he will differ from him in the matter of determining the nature of our being.[7] As will be recalled, for Descartes we are a "thinking substance." Locke disagrees with the two aspects of the Cartesian conception: the substantial nature of the self and that it always thinks.

We shall examine Locke's attitude in both cases, beginning with the second but paying special attention to the substantial element, for the main concern of this historical part, as has already been noted, lies in tracing the dissolutive process of the idea of substance, which culminates in Hume's thesis and gives rise to the opposite extreme of the fallacious dilemma stated in the preface.

For Descartes the uninterrupted continuity of thought in the res cogitans followed necessarily a priori. For, if the principal attribute of the res cogitans is thought, which constitutes its nature and essence, the thinking substance must uninterruptedly have the attribute of thought lest it cease to be a thinking substance. For Locke, on the other hand, the problem is a question of fact: "We know certainly, by experience, that we *sometimes* think . . . But whether that substance *perpetually* thinks or no, we can be no further assured than experience informs us." [8] The proposition that the soul is al-

7. The certainty of our knowledge has reference only to the *existence* of the self not to its nature; Locke expressly states this, writing that "we must content ourselves in the ignorance of what *kind* of being it is." (*Ibid.*, IV, iii, 6, p. 197.) Locke ignored the problem of the nature of the self in the first edition; in the second he added a chapter on the subject.

8. *Ibid.*, II, i, 10.

ways thinking is not self-evident, and to postulate, without qualifications, that thought is essential to it, adds Locke, is to beg the question, for one cannot use as proof the very hypothesis that is under discussion.

Having rejected the possibility of an a priori proof, Locke scrutinizes the various empirical situations and comes to the conclusion that there is as much reason to state that the soul is always thinking as there is to believe that a clock is thinking when it moves its pendulum. Locke maintains that there can be no thought unless we are conscious of it and that it is obvious that we are not conscious of having thought, or even of having dreamed, upon many occasions when we have been sleeping soundly. If a sleeping person thinks without realizing it, he is a different person than when he is awake, for consciousness is what constitutes personal identity.[9] Moreover, adds Locke, if I think without knowing it, how can another person know that I am thinking?[1] He concludes that thought is to the soul what movement is to the body—not its essence but one of its "operations."[2]

Locke's conception of substance is one of the more complex points of the *Essay*, and more than one reader has lost his bearings, I think, because this view sometimes seems self-contradictory. In certain passages we find Locke openly rejecting the idea of substance and even making fun of it; in others, quite the contrary, he not only defends it but accepts it as a logical necessity. Despite all the apparent contradictions, one fact is undeniable—

9. *Ibid.*, II, i, 11.
1. *Ibid.*, II, i, 17.
2. *Ibid.*, II, i, 10.

the dissolution of the substantialist conception is initiated in his *Essay*. However true it may be that its author could not shake himself completely free of all the ties that bound modern thought to substantialism, his contribution cannot be ignored by anyone concerned with what happened to the idea of substance. In the following paragraphs we shall examine the diversity of connotations attached to the idea of substance in Locke's *Essay* so as finally to make clear his contribution to the process of its dissolution.

It will perhaps facilitate the understanding of Locke's complex conception if one notes from the very beginning that in the *Essay* he is not concerned with substance but with the *idea* of substance and that one must be very careful, if one wishes to understand his thought as he himself expressed it, not to carry over into the ontological sphere his observations of an epistemological nature. A second warning is that one should separate, in Locke's doctrine, the idea of substance in general from the idea of particular substances.

The reader's first impression upon looking into the *Essay* is that Locke is completely rejecting the idea of substance as nothing more than "an uncertain supposition." [3] This attitude seems clear and consistent with his whole system, for the idea of substance cannot be innate [4] (there are no innate ideas) nor do we acquire it by either of the two legitimate means by which ideas can be acquired: sensation and reflection.

3. *Ibid.*, I, iii, 19.
4. *Ibid.*

Within this line of development, Locke considers that the idea of substance has little use in philosophy, being merely the result of a fallacy which consists of confusing words with things.[5] If one makes a thorough examination of what constitutes our idea of substance in general, says Locke, it will be discovered that it is a matter of a pre-supposition, of an unknown nature, that supports the qualities which are able to produce simple ideas in us and which are, in traditional language, called accidents.[6] Thus we have no idea of what substance is but only a "confused, obscure one of what it does,"[7] that is, that it supports accidents.

The statement that it supports accidents tells us nothing about the nature of the supposed substance. For Locke it is just something vague, similar to the notion held by the Hindu when he said that an elephant held up the earth and was held up in turn by a tortoise; when asked what held the tortoise up, he answered, "Something, I know not what."[8] Like the Hindu, we are fooling ourselves with the idea of substance or are acting like children who give the name "something" to whatever they cannot satisfactorily explain.[9]

All that has been observed so far has reference to the idea of substance in general and not to the ideas of particular substances, which is actually the problem that

5. Cf. *ibid.*, II, xiii, 18.
6. Cf. *ibid.*, II, xxiii, 2.
7. Cf. *ibid.*, II, xiii, 19.
8. Cf. *ibid.*; and II, xxiii, 2.
9. Cf. *ibid.*, II, xxiii, 2.

bothers Locke more and to which he devotes the greater
portion of the long chapter xxiii, Book II, of the *Essay*.
The problem of the idea of substance in general seems not
to have bothered him at first, for it is a subject that does
not come up in the first draft of the *Essay*.[1] Later on he
added several important paragraphs to the beginning of
chapter xxiii, Book II.

Although he denies that we have a clear, distinct idea
of substance in general, Locke does attempt to explain where our vague conception comes from. He believes that we arrive at it by abstracting the common element from various ideas of particular substances.[2] The
ideas of particular substances, in turn, are not formed by
a process of abstraction but arise from the observation
that an aggregate of simple ideas presents itself repeatedly
in the same form.[3]

In other words, ideas of particular substances are merely
modes of grouping simple ideas. Thus he defines them as
"a collection of a certain number of simple ideas, considered as united in one thing."[4]

The process by which such ideas are formed is a similar
one, whether it is a matter of material or immaterial substances, and the degree of clarity is about the same in

1. Cf. *An Early Draft of Locke's Essay*, ed. Aaron and Gibb.
2. Thus the abstract nature of substance in general. In his
"First Letter to Stillingfleet," Locke writes: "I must take the
liberty to deny there is any such thing *in rerum natura* as a general
substance that exists itself or makes anything."
3. Cf. *Essay*, II, xxiii, 1.
4. Cf. *ibid.*, II, xxiii, 14.

both cases.[5] In the specific case of what Locke calls "immaterial spirit," with which we are concerned here, the idea is formed as the result of the convergence of the simple ideas that come from reflection, such as thought, perception, etc.

By way of the so-called particular substances Locke returns to what he had criticized before, the idea of substance, and paves the way for an attitude that seems inconsistent with the one which we have seen so far. The ambiguity of his attitude is due, on the one hand, to the desire to break with the traditional idea of substance when he sees that his theory of knowledge has no place for such an idea [6] and, on the other hand, to his unwillingness to carry his initial epistemological attitude to its logical conclusion, either for fear of being accused of skepticism [7] or because the substantialist prejudice was still too deeply rooted in his habits of thought.[8]

Locke gives the impression that he is erasing with his elbow what he writes with his hand. He takes advantage of

5. Cf. *ibid.*, II, xxiii, 15.

6. If the ideas that we get by means of sensation and reflection are as far as our minds can reach (cf. *ibid.*, II, xxiii, 29), one cannot see how the idea of substance can legitimately be reintroduced since it originates in neither of those two ways. If it is answered that ideas of relationships are never the content of sensation or reflection, I should reply that in that case the idea arises as the result of an act of comparison between two different terms while in the case of substance there is but one term.

7. Cf. "First Letter to Stillingfleet," pp. 32–3.

8. Cf. "Third Letter to Stillingfleet," which we shall later comment upon; and *Essay*, II, xxiii, 4.

the distinction between the epistemological and ontological spheres in order to escape into the former when
attacked as a skeptic in the latter, never noticing that his
epistemology implicitly brings along with it an ontology
incompatible with the traditional one. In his reply to
Stillingfleet, bishop of Worcester, for example, he seems
to be a lawyer who is trying to find an ingenious alibi
rather than a revolutionary philosopher whose sole desire
is to follow the truth wherever it may lead. Here are his
words:

> It is laid to my charge that I look at the *being* of
> substance to be doubtful; and rendered it so by the
> imperfect and ill-grounded idea I have of it. To
> which I beg leave to say that I ground not the *being*
> but the *idea* of substance, on our accustoming our-
> selves to suppose some *substratum:* for it is of the
> *idea* alone that I speak there, and not of the *being* of
> substance. And having everywhere affirmed and built
> upon it, that *man* is a substance, I cannot be sup-
> posed to question or doubt of the being of substance.
> Further, I say that sensation convinces us that there
> *are solid and extended substances,* and reflection that
> there *are thinking substances.* So that I think the
> being of substance is not shaken by what I have said.[9]

Once he has made these concessions, it is easy for him
to pass from the conception of substance as an unknown
support—which he has made fun of—to the conception
of substance as a logical necessity. In his "Third Letter

9. "First Letter to Stillingfleet," p. 18.

to Stillingfleet" he supports the position that "there is substance, *because we cannot conceive how qualities should subsist by themselves.*" And he adds that "Sensible qualities carry the supposition of substance along with them . . . By carrying with them a supposition, I mean that sensible qualities *imply* a substratum to exist in." [1]

This belief in the impossibility of conceiving that qualities may exist per se [2] shows, even more than does his simple affirmation of the existence of extended and thinking substances, how far Locke was from having freed himself of the substantialist presupposition.[3]

Consequently it cannot surprise us when he defines the soul or "immaterial spirit" in terms that are similar to Descartes's, that is, as "a substance that thinks," adding that it "has a power of exciting motion in body, by

1. Cf. "Third Letter to Stillingfleet," Locke's italics. See also his *Essay*, II, xxiii, 4.

2. The expression, "We cannot conceive how qualities should subsist alone," which I have already cited, had appeared earlier in the *Essay* (II, xxiii, 4): "Because we cannot conceive how they should subsist alone, nor one in another, we suppose them existing in and supported by some common subject; which support we denote by the name substance . . ." His prejudice here seems attenuated by his use of the term "we suppose," which is the equivalent of the expression used in II, xxiii, 1, "We accustom ourselves to suppose some *substratum* . . ." Nevertheless, in the above-mentioned "Third Letter," he explains what he means by "supposition" in these words: "By carrying with them a supposition, I mean that sensible qualities *imply* a substratum to exist in."

3. On the substantialist presupposition, see above, p. 10 n. 2.

willing, or thought." [4] And he even goes as far as to assume an attitude similar to that of the Hindu he had made fun of. "We have in us *something* that thinks . . . though we must content ourselves in the ignorance of what *kind* of being it is." [5]

2. The problem of personal identity

The reader will be surprised again when, after having read these passages about the soul as a substance that thinks, he goes on to read Locke's discussion of the problem of personal identity. This is a simple matter for one who has a substantialist concept. Personal identity is based securely upon substantial identity. Locke does not, however, choose this way out. He makes a detailed study of the various meanings of the concept of identity in a long chapter [6] included in the second edition at the suggestion of Molyneux, who desired an amplification of Locke's ideas on the *principium individuationis*.[7]

Locke begins with the identity of inorganic matter. He shows that individual identity consists in the continuity of existence; this continuity, in turn, depends upon time and space, "we never finding, nor conceiving it possible, that two things of the same kind [8] should exist in the

4. *Essay*, II, xxiii, 22. Cf. *ibid.*, II, xxvii, 9.

5. Cf. *ibid.*, IV, iii, 6; I, i, 10. Later, in his *Examination of Malebranche*, para. 46, he maintains that reflection results in knowledge not of the mind but only of its operations.

6. *Essay*, II, xxvii.

7. Cf. Locke's letters to Molyneux dated Aug. 23, 1693, and March 8, 1695.

8. The qualification "of the same kind" is necessary because,

same place at the same time." [9] Likewise it is impossible for the same thing to exist in different places at the same time. And if one traces each thing back to its very beginning, one can establish the principle that "one thing cannot have two beginnings of existence, nor two things one beginning." [1]

The validity of this judgment seems to be unquestionable, according to Locke, when it is a matter of the identity of immutable physical substances such as the atom, as he understood the term, or a group or sum of atoms. But as soon as we try to apply this to other types of beings, such as plants, animals, or persons, we find that identity in these cases consists not in the permanence of the group of the same immutable particles but in something else. Thus, in the case of plants or animals the gain or loss of atoms does not alter identity. An oak tree, for example, is the same oak tree through all the stages of its development despite the fact that it grows and loses parts; the same thing can be said of a horse or any other animal.[2]

---

as we shall see, Locke considers that a finite mind and a body can occupy the same place at the same time.

9. *Essay*, II, xxvii, 1.

1. *Ibid.*

2. Cf. *ibid.*, II, xxvii, 3. In A. Campbell Fraser's edition, from which I quote, this paragraph appears erroneously as para. 4 (1, 441). In this edition, excellent in all other respects, there is an error in the numbering of paras. 3–10 in chap. xxvii of Bk. II of which the reader should be aware in order to avoid misunderstandings. This error begins when Fraser numbers the subparagraph entitled "Identity of Modes and Relations" para. 3 (1, 441) which actually forms part of para. 2, despite its independent title,

The identity of living beings is different from and independent of the particles of matter that constitute them. The identity of a plant or animal consists in the continuity

---

which is perhaps what caused the error. From the numbers of the paragraphs that follow, therefore, through para. 9, one unit must be subtracted in order to obtain the correct numeration.

With para. 10 (1, 447) another error in numbering begins. Para. 8, which Fraser considers para. 9 (1, 445) for the above-mentioned reason, is entitled "Same Man." After a long quotation Locke repeats the title of the paragraph without giving it a number, but Fraser makes it para. 10. When he comes to the following paragraph, which is actually para. 9, Fraser goes on numbering and makes it para. 11 (1, 448). He then drops the two extra numbers which he picked up, over and above the correct enumeration, and calls the following paragraph number 10, which is actually the correct number. But this creates considerable confusion in Fraser's edition since there are two paragraphs numbered 10 (on pp. 447 and 450 respectively). The same thing happens when para. 11 (p. 452) appears for the second time; though this time the number is correct, it increases the reader's confusion as he has already seen another para. 11 on p. 448. Thus, in order to correct the paragraph numbers, one must subtract one (1) from paras. 3–9 inclusive; para. 10 (p. 447) is the last part of para. 8 and para. 11 (p. 448) is actually para. 9. From para. 10 (p. 450) on, the numeration is correct.

These corrections are made on the basis of a comparison of numerous editions, including the three first editions of the *Essay* found in the Rare Book Room of the Sterling Memorial Library at Yale University. As we already know, this chapter did not appear in the first edition, published in London, 1690; it was added to the second edition. In this edition (1694) and the third (1695), published under the surveillance of Locke himself, the paragraphs of this chapter appear with the enumeration which I give above.

of the same "organization of parts in one coherent body, partaking of one common life." [3] It continues to be the same living being as long as it partakes of the same life, although the particles of matter that are incorporated into this living organization may be new and different. The particles of matter or atoms are of little importance in themselves; their significance depends upon the living relationship which they maintain with the whole.

We cannot, therefore, explain all types of identities by unity of substance; each kind of being has a kind of identity that is proper to it. [4]

Locke's departure from the substantialist interpretation is even greater when he turns his full attention to the problem of personal identity. According to him, personal identity is due not to the identity of substance but merely to the identity of consciousness. [5] Thought is always accompanied by consciousness of the fact that we are thinking. It is "impossible for any one to perceive without *perceiving* that he does perceive. When we see, hear,

3. *Essay*, II, xxvii, 4.
4. Cf. *ibid.*, II, xxvii, 7.
5. Cf. *ibid.*, II, xxvii, 23. The term "consciousness," referring to the apprehension by the self of its own operations and states, began to be used in Great Britain among the Cartesians and then by Locke; the word *conscientia* had, however, long been common among the Latin authors (cf. Cicero *Epistulae*, lib. VI, ep. iv). Locke does not distinguish between natural, direct consciousness and the reflexive act of explicit recognition by the self. Actually, the term "consciousness"—which appears so frequently in chap. xxvii, which was added to the second edition—is found almost nowhere in the rest of the work, with the exception of II, i, 10–19.

smell, taste, feel, meditate, or will anything, we know that we do so." [6] The consciousness that such "thoughts" belong to us is what constitutes what we call the self, "it not being considered, in this case, whether the same self be continued in the same or divers substances." [7]

The consciousness of the self is not limited solely to the present situation but also reaches back into the past. "This personality extends itself beyond present existence to what is past, only by consciousness . . . ; owns and imputes to itself past actions just upon the same ground and for the same reason as it does the present." [8]

Personal identity, then, consists in consciousness, "which is inseparable from thought."

Locke is quite explicit with regard to the fact that personal identity has nothing to do with substantial identity. "Personal identity consists: not in the identity of substance, but, as I have said, in the identity of consciousness." [9] And further on he reaffirms this concept when he writes that "nothing but consciousness can unite remote existences into the same person: the identity of substance will not do it . . . It is evident the personal identity would be equally determined by the consciousness, whether that consciousness were annexed to some individual immaterial substance or no." [1]

6. Cf. *ibid.*, II, xxvii, 9 (para. 11 in Fraser's ed., 1, 448–9).
7. *Ibid.*
8. *Ibid.*, II, xxvii, 26.
9. *Ibid.*, II, xxvii, 19.
1. *Ibid.*, II, xxvii, 23; cf. also paras. 14, 16, 17, 21, 25.

Different substances, by the same consciousness (where they do partake in it) [are] united into one person, as well as different bodies by the same life are united into one animal, whose identity is preserved in that change of substances by the unity of one continued life. For, it being the same consciousness that makes a man be himself to himself, personal identity depends on [2] that only, whether it be annexed solely to one individual substance, or can be continued in a succession of several substances.[3]

The identity of the self is so completely dependent upon the subject's consciousness of past and present states that to deny this identity because of the time that has intervened between one state and another or because of the change of substance is as absurd as claiming that someone is not the same person because he is "wearing other clothes today than he did yesterday" or because his present state is separated from yesterday's "with a long or a short sleep between: the same consciousness uniting those distant actions into the same person, whatever substances contributed to their production." [4]

The fact that in this paragraph Locke is referring princi-

2. In the other passages he had stated not that personal identity "depends on" but that it "is constituted by" consciousness. But in both cases, consciousness does not merely discover personal identity; it constitutes it.

3. *Essay*, II, xxvii, 10 (ed. Fraser, 1, 450–1).

4. *Ibid.*

pally to material substance is proved by the content of
the following paragraph [5] and its connection with the
one which we have been studying. In paragraph 11 Locke
analyzes what causes a hand to belong to a person and
comes to the conclusion that it is consciousness and not
the material constitution of the hand. If we cut off someone's hand, it ceases to belong to him because, having
been affected by other bodies, it is no longer able to affect the self's consciousness as it used to when it was
joined to the rest of the organism. At the same time, the
identity of the person is kept intact despite the loss of
the hand.

Locke then passes immediately to the most vital problem, that of the relationship of personal identity to the
identity of the immaterial substance. He states the problem on the basis of two questions: *a*) Does one remain
the same person if "the substance that thinks" changes?
And *b*), Can there be different persons in a substance
that never changes? [6] Locke maintains that question *a*
can be answered only by those who are aware of what
sort of substance it is that thinks and who know whether
the consciousness of past actions can be transferred from
one thinking substance to another. And he adds that if
the same consciousness can be transferred from one thinking substance to another it is possible that two thinking
substances may constitute a single person. "For the same
consciousness being preserved, whether in the same or

5. *Ibid.*, II, xxvii, 11 (ed. Fraser, 1, 452).
6. Cf. *ibid.*, II, xxvii, 12.

different substances, the personal identity is preserved." [7]

With regard to question *b*, Locke repeats once more that personal identity depends upon consciousness and not upon substance. If someone maintains that his soul or immaterial substance is that of Nestor, Socrates, or any other person who no longer exists, the only way to determine whether the self of the person who makes this claim is the same as that of the absent person is to find out whether he feels that the actions of Nestor or Socrates are his very own. If not, he has no more reason to claim that he is that person than he would have if some part of Nestor's or Socrates' body now constituted a part of his body, "the same immaterial substance, without the same consciousness, no more making the same person, by being united to any body, than the same particle of matter, without consciousness, united to any body, makes the same person." [8]

What has been stated so far has reference to the identity of the person but can be applied equally well to the identity of the self, for both terms have the same denotation for Locke, though they differ in connotation. Self is the person as it sees itself, and person is the self seen from outside. I am self only for myself and am person for other persons.[9] It is this difference in point of view that obliges Locke to make a distinction between the definitions of self and of person. Person he defines as "a thinking, in-

7. *Ibid.*, II, xxvii, 13.
8. *Ibid.*, II, xxvii, 14.
9. Cf. *ibid.*, II, xxvii, 26.

telligent being" [1] and self as "a conscious, thinking thing." [2]

Locke makes a distinction between the ideas of "self" and "person" and the idea of "man." The "man" is made up not of soul alone but also of "body and shape." [3] If the soul of a prince, with consciousness of his past, were united with the body of a shoemaker whose soul had left it, there is no doubt, says Locke, that the prince's "person" would live on; but the same could not be said of the "man," for the body, too, constitutes part of the idea of the "man." For everyone except the prince himself, who sees himself from the inside, the "man" continues to be the shoemaker. [4] If the same man, adds Locke,

1. "Thinking intelligent being, that has reason and reflection, and can consider itself as itself, the same thinking thing, in different times and places." *Ibid.*, II, xxvii, 9 (in Fraser's ed., 1, 448, it appears erroneously as 11; cf. above, p. 33 n. 2).

2. "*Self* is that conscious thinking thing,—whatever substance made up of, (whether spiritual or material, simple or compounded, it matters not)—which is sensible or conscious of pleasure and pain, capable of happiness or misery." *Essay*, II, xxvii, 17.

As can be seen in these two definitions, Locke is deliberately avoiding the use of the term "substance" by replacing it with "being" and "thing"; but he still cannot free himself from the concept of substance as the support of the qualities which he attributes to the "being" and to the "thing."

3. *Ibid.*, II, xxvii, 7.

4. *Ibid.*, II, xxvii, 15. As may be seen by the example cited, Locke takes seriously the view of the soul as a total being separable from the body, hence his analysis of situations derived from possible reincarnations of the soul in different bodies. Cf. *ibid.*, II, xxvii, 7.

could have more than one distinct, incommunicable consciousness, he would constitute different persons at different moments within a single body.[5] In reply to the difficulties that arise from the attempt to determine the identity of the "man," [6] Locke repeats his conclusion that personal identity can be derived only from the continuity of consciousness.[7]

3. The conflict between the empirical method and the substantialist presupposition

After insisting to the point of becoming wearisome that "the self is not determined by identity or diversity of substance . . . , but only by identity of consciousness," [8] he surprises us by suddenly shifting his position and stating that he considers as "the more probable opinion, that this consciousness is annexed to, and the affection of, one individual immaterial substance." [9]

This fluctuation of attitudes, which characterizes the instability of Locke with regard to the problem of substance, becomes disconcerting for the reader who is looking for a consistent, systematic position, forgetting the

5. *Ibid.*, II, xxvii, 20.
6. Locke considers three possibilities without clearly defining his position. The identity of the "man" may depend upon the fact that it keeps *a*) the same thinking, immaterial substance, i.e. the same soul; *b*) the same body; or *c*) the same immaterial spirit joined to the same body. Cf. *ibid.*, II, xvii, 21.
7. *Ibid.*
8. *Ibid.*, II, xxvii, 23.
9. *Ibid.*, II, xxvii, 25.

historical circumstances under which Locke's work was written. The instability referred to is not, in my opinion, an accidental matter but the result of a deep inner conflict between the "historical experimental method" which he initiated and the metaphysical presuppositions which continued to influence him. His method—and, in general, his whole epistemology—leaves no room for the idea of substance, but his philosophical training within substantialism [1] has left him with a set of metaphysical prejudices and, in particular, with the belief that substance is a logical necessity.[2] The presence of these two opposing forces can be seen on two different levels. The more superficial level, and the one which first attracts the reader's attention, can be noted when the substantialist presupposition emerges in the midst of an epistemological investigation and leads Locke astray from the implications of his method; or when, in the midst of a substantialistic argument, his line of reasoning is abruptly interrupted by the reappearance of his epistemological principles.[3] On a deeper level the conflict between the two tendencies may be seen in an ambiguity in his words. Thus, whenever he

1. It should be kept in mind that the influence which shaped him most basically was that of Descartes and that the embryonic empiricism of his fellow countryman Bacon did not in the least affect him.

2. Cf. *Essay*, II, xxiii, 4; and the "Third Letter to Stillingfleet," quoted above, p. 31 n. 1.

3. A typical example of this attitude is the passage in which he admits substance as a logical necessity and then adds in the following line that he is sure that we do not have a very clear idea of what we mean by substance. See *Essay*, II, xxiii, 4.

is expressly repudiating the substantialist conception his words tend to become meaningless, and he ends by making a verbal repudiation or by becoming involved in linguistic sleight of hand so as to avoid the use of the term "substance" in his definitions.[4] On other occasions quite the opposite happens. Locke expressly recognizes the necessity for substance, but he is so betrayed by what he says that substance is transformed into an empty notion, deprived of all content and meaning.

In the first case, his repudiation of substantialism becomes a mere pose as he uses new words to conceal the same old content; in the second case, the skeletal remnant of substantialism becomes more and more shadowy until all that is left is the verbal adhesion to an empty, meaningless term.

One can clearly observe the existence and meaning of Locke's ambiguous attitude and, at the same time, the gradual decay of the substantialist idea by comparing his views with those of Descartes. In the case of both men, substantialism is assumed, but whereas the French philosopher constructs his whole system upon the basis of the concept of substance and has an epistemology that supports his metaphysics, the author of the *Essay* keeps substance as a sort of vestigial organ, a useless appendage,

4. Such is the case with regard to his definitions of "person" and "self," which appear at the very height of his attack upon the idea of substance, whether material or immaterial. Cf. *Essay*, II, xxvii, 9 (ed. Fraser, para. 11, p. 448) and 17. As will be recalled, he replaces the word "substance" in one case by "being" and in the other by "thing."

and develops a system which not only does not need the idea of substance but implicitly contradicts it. His theory of knowledge reveals the flimsiness of substantialism when it is examined in the light of an empirical method and shows that substance was really nothing more than an unknowable presupposition.[5]

Once the concept of substance had been reduced to the status of Locke's meaningless "I-know-not-what," it was an obvious step for his immediate successors to dispense with it altogether. It shows a lack of historical perspective to deny Locke's contribution to the process of substantialism's decay, which is evident when we compare the philosophers who followed him, who actually could not have been what they were if the author of the *Essay* had not previously opened the way for them.

A point which is not explicitly developed by Locke but which is perhaps one of his most important contributions

5. Cf. *ibid.*, II, xxiii, 2. Locke seems to have conceived of the idea of substance from the very beginning as a presupposed substratum that is unknowable. In a draft of the *Essay* he wrote: "it is evident that haveing noe other Idea or notion of body but something wherein those many sensible qualitys which affect our senses doe subsist, by supposeing a substance wherein thinking knowing doubting hopeing feareing &c. doe subsist we have as cleare a notion of the essence of a spirit as any one hath of the essence of body, the one being supposd to be without knowing what it is the substratum to those simple Ideas that we receive from without and the other supposd (with a like ignorance of what it is) to be the substratum to those actions we experiment in our selves within." *An Early Draft of Locke's Essay*, ed. Aaron and Gibb, p. 7.

to the overthrow of substantialism is the fact that of the two senses in which the concept of substance could be taken—*res per se subsistens* and *substans accidentibus*—Locke chose the second; this greatly facilitated the process of the disintegration of substance. Let us consider only one of a number of other possibilities. What would have happened to Berkeley's criticism, which contributed so much to this disintegration process on the basis of Locke's treatment of the problem, if the latter had considered substance as a res per se subsistens? But as it was, since he had taken the concept of substance in its other sense, as a support for accidents, the process was immensely facilitated.

In retrospect, we may sum it all up in a few words. The substans accidentibus was changed by Locke into a meaningless, unknowable point of reference for qualities; with Berkeley it disappeared completely from the realm of matter; and Hume demonstrated its nonexistence and uselessness in the spiritual sphere.

It is no accident that Continental rationalism took substance almost exclusively in the sense of a res per se subsistens and, with Spinoza, reached its conclusion by identifying substance with God. This was the process of the unification of Descartes's substantialism. In the British Isles, on the other hand, there was a process of disintegration, which we are tracing in this historical section and which now leads us to the examination of Berkeley's views.

CHAPTER III

Berkeley on Material and Spiritual Substance

1. Berkeley and Locke

Berkeley represents another stage in the disintegration of the concept of the res cogitans. This is not because he attacked this concept but because his famous criticism of general abstract ideas and of matter undermined the substantiality of the spirit by allowing Hume to apply to the substantial identity of the self the same arguments that Berkeley had used to get rid of corporeal substance.

Berkeley's attitude with regard to substance is even more contradictory and paradoxical than Locke's. While carrying to its ultimate consequences the critical process of destroying the idea of substance in the material realm, he defends this idea in the spiritual sphere by means of the same conceptual apparatus that he had formerly criticized. We shall study the various stages of this process by taking as our point of departure his criticism of general abstract ideas, which connects him with Locke and serves as the basis of his immaterialism.

It cannot be doubted that Berkeley had been steeped in the atmosphere of ideas aroused by the publication of the *Essay Concerning Human Understanding* when he wrote the three works that are pertinent to the development of my thesis.[1] This is proved not only by the numerous quotations from and references to Locke in his *Principles* [2] but also by the fact that the first book of notes written in his youth [3] shows that he wrote them while reading the *Essay*.

1. *An Essay Towards a New Theory of Vision* (1709); *A Treatise Concerning the Principles of Human Knowledge* (1710); *Three Dialogues Between Hylas and Philonous* (1713).

2. Especially in the introduction; cf. secs. 11, 13, 18, and *passim*. The first draft of the introduction, written in 1708, shows even better than the published version the connection between Berkeley's ideas and the *Essay*.

3. Bk. B, which together with Bk. A forms what is known as the *Commonplace Book*, first published by A. C. Fraser in 1871. Theodor Lorenz has demonstrated that the two books of notes, which are in the British Museum (Add. Ms. 39305), were bound together in the wrong sequence; Bk. B, therefore, is prior to A. Cf. his article in *Archiv für Geschichte der Philosophie*, 18 (1901), 551 ff. According to John Wild, Berkeley wrote Bk. B toward the end of 1707 and Bk. A in 1715 or 1716. Many other students of his writings believe that the two books were written one after the other with only a brief lapse of time between. Except for Hone and Rossi, everyone now accepts Lorenz' order. I shall quote from G. A. Johnston's edition (London, Faber and Faber, 1930), which unfortunately is not wholly reliable, as shown by R. I. Aaron in *Mind*, N.S., 11, No. 160, 455 ff. In Johnston's edition Bk. B includes numbers 1–395 and 903–53 and Bk. A. numbers 396–902. There is also a German edition by Andreas Hecht (Leipzig, Meiner, 1926) and a new one by A. A. Luce (London, T. Nelson, 1944).

The reader will understand the importance of this work in any serious attempt to trace the antecedents of Berkeley's ideas.

Locke's *Essay* had great repercussions and became very popular soon after its publication. Perhaps its popularity is due to the fact that it dealt with empirical matters and analyzed them in relatively simple language at a time when speculative discussions clothed in technical jargon were in preponderance. It did not, however, impress Berkeley as a model of clear language or empirical analysis when he read it almost 20 years after it had been published. In his judgment, the *Essay* was full of unjustified abstractions, circumlocutions, and linguistic imprecision. He comments that "Locke's great oversight seems to be that he did not begin with his third book," [4] which, as we know, treats of language. And he insists upon this when he writes: "Certainly the 2^d & 4th books don't agree with wt he says in ye 3^d." [5] Berkeley believes that the greatest defect in the *Essay* is that words are substituted for concrete objects.[6] A typical example of such verbalism and abstraction is Locke's famous "general triangle," which Berkeley subjects to severe criticism in his *Principles*. In one of his last notes he writes of the necessity for dealing the "general triangle" its coup de grâce.[7]

This insistence upon such points, which we find in his first book of notes, shows that the critical portion of the *Principles* is intimately bound up with Berkeley's reaction

4. *Commonplace Book*, ed. Johnston, No. 729.
5. *Ibid.*
6. *Ibid.*, Nos. 560, 601, 645, 647.
7. *Ibid.*, No. 699: "Mem. To bring the killing blow at the last, *e.g.*, in the matter of abstraction to bring Locke's general triangle in the last."

to Locke's viewpoint. The impression made upon him by the *Essay's* abstraction and verbalism shows that he had conceived of his own position, from the very beginning, as concrete logic and true empiricism in contrast to Locke's logic of symbols and pseudo empiricism.

In his *Treatise Concerning the Principles of Human Knowledge,* which is a basic document in the study of such problems as those discussed in this book, Berkeley felt it necessary to clear the ground before undertaking to build a positive system. This first critical task is perhaps Berkeley's greatest contribution to modern philosophy, and it has been so recognized by those concerned with carrying on his work.[8]

2. Criticism of general abstract ideas

Berkeley begins with a criticism of the opinion that we are capable of forming abstract ideas, a belief which in his judgment "seems to have had a chief part in rendering speculation intricate and perplexed, and to have occasioned innumerable errors and difficulties in almost all parts of knowledge." [9]

8. Cf. Hume's words at the beginning of sec. vii, Pt. I of Bk. I, of his *Treatise of Human Nature:* "A great philosopher has disputed the received opinion in this particular, and has asserted, that all general ideas are nothing but particular ones . . . As I look upon this to be one of the greatest and most valuable discoveries that has been made of late years in the republic of letters, I shall here endeavour to confirm it by some arguments, which I hope will put it beyond all doubt and controversy."

9. A *Treatise Concerning the Principles of Human Knowledge,* sec. 6 of introduction. In sec. 17 of the same he writes of "the false

In the rough draft of the introduction to the *Principles* Berkeley tells us what he means by abstract idea. He writes:

> By abstract idea, genera, species, universal notions, all which amount to the same thing, as I find these terms explain'd by the best and clearest writers, we are to understand ideas which equally represent the particulars of any sort, and are made by the mind, which, observing that the individuals of each kind agree in some things and differ in others, takes out and singles from the rest, that which is common to all, making thereof one abstract general idea; which contains all those ideas wherein the particulars of that kind agree, separated from and exclusive of all those other concomitant ideas, whereby they are distinguished one from another. To this abstract general idea thus framed the mind gives a general name, and lays it up and uses it as a standard whereby to judge what particulars are and what are not to be accounted of that sort, those onely which contain every part of the general idea having a right to be admitted into that sort and called by that name.[1]

In this passage Berkeley does not, as G. A. Johnston erroneously maintains, identify general ideas with genera,

Principles that have obtained in the world; amongst all which there is none, methinks, hath a more wide influence over the thoughts of speculative men than this of *abstract general ideas*."

　1. *The Works of George Berkeley*, ed. A. C. Fraser, 3 (Oxford, Clarendon Press, 1901), 360. Except where otherwise indicated I shall quote from this edition.

species, and universal notions, for he makes reference not to his own conception but to the use made of such terms by "the best and clearest writers." Nor does he deny, as the same noted critic again erroneously argues, the universal element in knowledge.[2] It is true that Berkeley is sometimes careless in expressing himself, but the context of both the *Commonplace Book* and the *Principles* reveals that he is criticizing not universals in general or "general ideas" but only "abstract general ideas." In the *Principles* he states explicitly: "And here it is to be noted that I do not deny absolutely there are *general ideas*, but only that there are any *abstract general ideas*." [3]

2. G. A. Johnston in his well-known work, *The Development of Berkeley's Philosophy* (London, Macmillan, 1923), writes that in the rough draft referred to "Berkeley denied entirely the universal element in Knowledge" (p. 119) and that "his criticism is perfectly general, and is directed against 'genera, species, universal notions, all of which amount to the same thing' " (*ibid.*). As may be easily seen, Johnston distorts Berkeley's thought by quoting him out of context; he ignores what follows, "as I find these terms explained by the best and clearest writers."

It is obvious that later on Berkeley did not deny this universal element. He writes in the *Principles*, for example: "It is, I know, a point much insisted on, that all knowledge and demonstration are about universal notions, to which I fully agree." Introd., sec. 15.

3. *Principles*, introd., sec. 12. It is true that in the *Commonplace Book* he writes that there are no general ideas (ed. Johnston, No. 397), but it should be noted that Berkeley is careless with his language in these notes. Cf. ed. Johnston, No. 597. In this edition, Johnston, though interpreting the meaning correctly, sometimes makes the mistake of putting "abstract general idea"

As can be seen from the long passage quoted above, the process of forming general ideas has two stages. First, we compare different individuals and apprehend what is common to them; second, we form an idea of the qualities common to them and exclude their other qualities. It never occurred to Berkeley to deny the validity of the first stage of the process. What he denied was that one could form an idea of the common quality in isolation from the other qualities.

In the introduction to his *Principles*, as it was published, Berkeley was more explicit about the process of forming abstract ideas of quality and beings. It is admitted, he writes, that although the qualities or modes of things do not exist separated from them the spirit is able to consider each quality in abstraction from the others and to form in this way an abstract idea of this quality. Thus it perceives an extended, colored, moving object and is able to reduce to its simple components this compound idea and, taking each quality separately, form the abstract ideas of extension, color, and movement.[4] This is not the only way of forming an abstract idea. Sometimes the spirit does not really separate one quality from the others in the same object but considers what is common to qualities that exist in different objects and forms an abstract idea of this quality. In this way we obtain the abstract idea of color, which is neither red, blue,

---

in place of Berkeley's expression, "abstract idea." (Cf. Nos. 499, 676.) See R. I. Aaron's article in *Mind*, cited above.

4. *Principles*, introd., sec. 7.

white, nor any other particular color.[5] Likewise abstract ideas are formed of more complex beings. When we observe a series of different human beings, for example, we do not pay attention to what is peculiar to each one of them but only retain an impression of what is common to them. Thus we arrive at the abstract idea of "man," which includes color, size, etc. but not a definite color and size, for the idea "man" includes black and white, tall and short, etc.[6]

Berkeley considers it impossible to arrive at such ideas; he, at least, is not capable of such abstractions. "The idea of man that I frame to myself must be either of a white, or a black, or a tawny, a straight, or a crooked, a tall, or a low, or a middle-sized man." [7] "I can imagine a man with two heads; or the upper part of a man joined to the body of a horse. I can consider the hand, the eye, the nose, each by itself abstracted or separated from the rest of the body. But then whatever hand or eye I imagine, it must have some particular shape and colour." [8] He admits that he can consider as separate particular qualities which, though they may exist united to others in the constitution of an object, can really exist in separation; but he does not believe that it is possible to conceive of qualities in isolation if they cannot exist in isolation, as is true in the case of color and extension.

In this examination and criticism of the possibility of

5. *Ibid.*, sec. 8.
6. *Ibid.*, sec. 9.
7. *Ibid.*, sec. 10.
8. *Ibid.*

abstraction such as he describes it, Berkeley constantly appeals to the reader to decide in accordance with his personal experience. This appeal to individual experience gives his whole discussion of abstract ideas an empirico-psychological emphasis, which is characteristic of the British attitude of that time. The fundamental terms of the discussion acquire a special meaning which restricts the problem to the psychological sphere. Section 10 of the introduction, referred to before, suffices to show what Berkeley understands by *idea, conceive,* and *abstract.* He begins, "Whether others have this wonderful faculty of *abstracting* their ideas, they best can tell. . . . I find indeed I have a faculty of *imagining,* or *representing* to myself, the ideas of those particular things I have perceived and of variously compounding and dividing them." [9] For him, to abstract or to conceive (terms that he uses synonymously in this section) is equivalent to imagining or representing to oneself.[1] And if abstraction has this meaning the discussion is ended, for it is evident that we cannot imagine a man who is simultaneously tall and short, black and white, young and old, etc.; nor can we imagine color separated from extension or movement in abstraction from the thing moving. Likewise, *idea* in this context is equivalent to *representation,* and again it is evident that we cannot have an "idea" of the above-mentioned objects.

9. *Ibid.,* italics mine.
1. In sec. 5 he writes: "I imagine the trunk of a human body without limbs, or conceive the smell of a rose without thinking on the rose itself."

In his polemic against abstract ideas, Berkeley chooses for his criticism Locke's famous "general triangle," which is neither oblique nor right angled, neither equilateral, isosceles, nor scalene, but all and none of them at the same time.[2] It is easy for him to demonstrate that we do not have an "idea" of such a triangle nor can we conceive of a figure with such disparate qualities.[3]

This attitude has led some critics to believe that Berkeley denies all forms of abstraction, considering them impossible and unnecessary. But this is not true. Berkeley admits that "a man may consider a figure merely as triangular; without attending to the particular qualities of the angles, or relations of the sides. *So far he may abstract.* But this will never prove that he can frame an abstract, general, inconsistent *idea* of a triangle. In like manner we may consider Peter so far forth as man, or so far forth as animal, without framing the forementioned abstract idea, either of man or of animal; inasmuch as all that is perceived is not considered." [4]

Although this passage was added to the second edition

2. Cf. Locke, *Essay Concerning Human Understanding,* IV, vii, 9.

3. Of course, Locke never maintained that the mind could imagine the idea of a triangle which was neither equilateral, isosceles, nor scalene, nor all three at the same time. Moreover, in the passage cited in the preceding note, with reference to the general idea of a triangle, he admits that "it is something imperfect, that cannot exist; [it is] an idea wherein some parts of several different and inconsistent ideas are put together." Cf. Locke, *Essay* (ed. Fraser, 2, 274).

4. *Principles,* introd., sec. 16.

of the *Principles* which was published 25 years after the
first one,[5] from his youth Berkeley had conceived of the
distinction between *considering* a quality in isolation and
forming an abstract idea of such a quality. He writes in
the *Commonplace Book* that there is "A great difference
between *considering* length without breadth, & having
an *idea* of, or *imagining* length without breadth." [6]
Berkeley uses the scholastic term "consider" quite frequently.[7] In his *Three Dialogues Between Hylas and
Philonous* he uses this term in the same sense. Philonous
says: "I acknowledge, Hylas, it is not difficult to form
general propositions and reasonings about those qualities,
without mentioning any other; and, in this sense, to consider or treat of them abstractedly." [8]

In conclusion, what Berkeley denies is that one can
form an idea of one quality to the exclusion of the others
or of an object which has contradictory and mutually exclusive qualities; but he admits that we can *consider* a
quality in abstraction from the others although we have
never actually perceived it in isolation.

Berkeley not only denies that we can form or conceive
of general abstract ideas but also maintains that these
ideas are meaningless.[9] Abstraction for him is a process

5. First ed., 1710; second, 1734.

6. *Commonplace Book*, ed. Johnston, No. 263.

7. Cf. St. Thomas Aquinas, *Summa Theologica*, I q. 85a. I
ad I.

8. *Dialogues*, I, ed. Fraser, 1, 403. Cf. similar usage in the two
letters which he wrote to Jean Leclerc, discovered and published
by Lorenz in *Archiv für Gesch. der Phil.*, 17, 159.

9. Cf. *Principles*, rough draft of introd., ed. Fraser, 3, 361.

of mutilating reality. Let us follow his line of reasoning as applied to his example, "man." The abstract idea of man, which is different from individual men and also from all the qualities which distinguish one man from another, is meaningless. Such a man *in abstracto* is neither black nor white nor yellow nor the combination of all these colors together. It may perhaps be claimed that he has a color in abstracto, but this means very little for it would be a colorless color. The moment it has definite color or a mixture of all the colors it ceases to be color in general and changes into a specific color. What has been said about his color can be said of the figure and other qualities of this general abstract man. Such a "man" does not, consequently, have color, size, shape, weight, or any other quality. He cannot even have arms, legs, eyes, nose, etc., for men can be found who do not have these members, and the general idea of man must include all individuals without exception. Each of these qualities that are abstracted amounts to a mutilation of man, who ends up by turning into pure nothingness, after having lost all the qualities which characterize men.[1]

Berkeley considers that the source of this vicious tendency of man toward abstract ideas is language.[2] As proof of this he cites "the plain confession of the ablest patrons of abstract ideas," [3] referring the reader to the *Essay Concerning Human Understanding*, III, vi, 39. Since "we are

1. *Ibid.*, pp. 360–1.
2. *Principles*, introd., secs. 18–20. Cf. rough draft, ed. Fraser, 3, 371–2.
3. *Principles*, introd., sec. 18.

apt to think every noun substantive stands for a distinct
idea that may be separated from all others," [4] when we
come across a word to which we cannot attribute a concrete idea we come to the conclusion that it must be a
general abstract idea.[5] Hence the existence, in both the
everyday and the philosophical vocabulary, of so many
words that are completely lacking in meaning. Then false
abstraction concludes by being mere empty verbalism.

3. Material substance

This long polemic against general abstract ideas—to
which Berkeley devotes practically all of the introduction
to his *Principles* besides passages in other writings [6]—constitutes a foundation for the attitude which he assumes
with regard to material substance, a problem which may
now be resolved in a few words, with no chance for misunderstandings to arise: matter or corporeal substance is
a general abstract idea and therefore has no existence.[7]

Berkeley is not content, however, to reject corporeal
substance on the basis of this argument alone.[8] Again he

4. *Ibid.*, sec. 116.
5. Cf. *Principles*, rough draft of introd., ed. Fraser, 3, 378.
6. In addition to secs. 6–20 in the introduction to the *Principles* and the numerous notes in the *Commonplace Book*, Berkeley devotes the following passages to the criticism of general abstract ideas: *An Essay Towards a New Theory of Vision*, sec. 123;
Alciphron, 7, 5; *Defense of Free Thinking in Mathematics*, secs.
45–8.
7. Cf. *Principles*, sec. 11.
8. The importance of the criticism of general abstract ideas as
a basis for the rejection of material substance is so great that

finds in Locke material for a critique which is today a classic of modern philosophy.

As will be recalled, Locke distinguishes between primary and secondary [9] qualities.[1] Primary qualities "are utterly inseparable from the body, in what state soever it be";[2] in this group are included solidity, extension, figure, mobility, and number. Secondary qualities "are nothing in the objects themselves but powers to produce various sensations in us by their primary qualities, i.e. by the bulk, figure, texture, and motion of their insensible parts."[3] These are sensible qualities, such as colors,

---

some scholars have explained the importance of Berkeley's immaterialism, in contrast to the brief and scant attention paid to the thought of Arthur Collier, by the fact that the latter did not base his immaterialistic thesis upon a previous nominalistic doctrine. Cf. A. A. Luce, *Berkeley and Malebranche* (London, Oxford University Press, 1934), p. 128.

9. In modern times we find a similar distinction in Descartes, Galileo, Hobbes, and Boyle. According to F. Pillon, Locke took this distinction from Descartes and his followers. On the other hand, C. A. Fraser believes that he took it from his friend Boyle, who even uses the same terms in his work, *Origin of Forms and Qualities* (Oxford, 1666).

1. Locke writes that "the power to produce any idea in our mind I call *quality* of the subject wherein that power is." *Essay*, II, viii, 8. Thus he names as qualities of a snowball its powers of producing in us the ideas of coldness, whiteness, and roundness.

2. *Essay*, II, viii, 9. Locke takes as an example a grain of wheat: however small particles it be divided into, each particle will still have solidity, extension, figure, and mobility.

3. *Essay*, II, viii, 10.

sounds, flavors, etc. The ideas that we have of primary qualities closely resemble the qualities as they really exist in the objects, whereas our ideas of secondary qualities are in no way similar to the qualities in the objects but are the impressions produced in us by the primary qualities of insensible particles.[4] In other words, whereas solidity, extension, etc. really exist in the objects odor, flavor, etc. exist not in the objects but only in ourselves. And in this sense they are considered subjective.

This distinction is of crucial importance in the formation of Berkeley's attitude with regard to material substance. In fact, his whole contribution consists in applying to primary qualities the subjectivity that Locke admitted in the case of the secondary qualities.[5] In this way, matter as a corporeal substance is dissolved into nothingness.

Berkeley begins by denying the distinction between primary and secondary qualities since he considers it impossible to conceive them separately. His argument is again of an empirico-psychological nature:

> But I desire any one to reflect, and try whether he can, by any abstraction of thought, conceive the extension and motion of a body without all other sensible qualities. For my own part, I see evidently that it is not in my power to frame an idea of a body extended and moving, but I must withal give it some colour or other sensible quality, which is acknowl-

4. *Essay*, II, viii, 15.
5. Cf. *Principles*, secs., 10, 15.

edged to exist only in the mind. In short, extension, figures, and motion, abstracted from all other qualities, are inconceivable. Where therefore the other sensible qualities are, there must these be also, to wit, in the mind and nowhere else.[6]

Thus we see that the same reasons that prove the subjectivity of secondary qualities serve also as proof of the subjective character of primary qualities.[7] It is freely admitted that heat and cold exist not in the corporeal substances that produce them but merely in the mind, for the same thing may seem hot to one hand and cold to the other. Thus, may one not also affirm the same concerning extension and figure, asks Berkeley, since these, too, appear to be different to the same eye when moved from point to point or to different eyes viewing the object from the very same point? Hence extension and figure cannot be the images of anything fixed and determinate unless it be something in the mind.[8] And "if *extension* be once acknowledged to have no existence without the mind, the same must necessarily be granted of motion, solidity, and gravity; since they all evidently suppose extension." [9] Thus one by one primary qualities are eliminated from the realm of objective existence.

The objection may perhaps be made that even though it be admitted that both primary and secondary qualities are subjective nothing has been proved concern-

6. *Ibid.,* sec. 10.
7. *Ibid.,* sec. 14.
8. *Ibid.;* and *Dialogues,* I, ed. Fraser, 1, 399.
9. *Dialogues,* 1, 401.

ing the validity or fallacy of corporeal *substance*, which must not be confused with qualities, whether considering them separately or all together. In anticipation of a possible objection of this sort, Berkeley launches into an examination of what corporeal substance means. Of the two meanings of the word "substance" Berkeley, following Locke, chooses the one according to which substance is considered that which supports accidents. "If we inquire into what the most accurate philosophers declare themselves to mean by *material substance*, we shall find them acknowledge they have no other meaning annexed to those sounds but the idea of Being in general, together with the relative notion of its supporting accidents." [1] He considers the idea of being in general as incomprehensible and abstract and does not know what meaning can be attached to the idea of "supporting," since it surely cannot have a usual or literal meaning. It makes no difference, however. Whatever the meaning attached to the material substratum or supporter of qualities, the admission of it implies the supposition that it has its own existence outside of the mind; and this is not only erroneous but contradictory and "wholly inconceivable." [2]

Berkeley wishes to pursue his criticism of material substance further and therefore, as a hypothesis, admits its existence; then he asks how we could know it if it actually existed. He believes that the only two roads to knowledge that we have are sense and reason. It seems certain that we

1. *Principles*, sec. 17.
2. *Ibid.*

cannot know the existence of the material substratum by the senses, since the senses can give us ideas only of concrete qualities; therefore we shall have to infer the existence of the substratum by reason on the basis of what is immediately perceived by the senses. But this also is impossible, for "the very patrons of Matter themselves do not pretend there is any necessary connexion betwixt them (bodies without the mind) and our ideas." [3]

Berkeley identifies matter as corporeal substance with "bodies without the mind," and his attack on substantiality frequently seems to arise from his desire to cut off realism's sole remaining possibility once the subjectivity of qualities has been demonstrated, this sole remaining possibility being, of course, to admit this subjectivity and at the same time to maintain the existence of a substance that is independent of the mind and serves as a substratum for qualities.

Berkeley believes that he has demonstrated that corporeal substance is a hypothesis, not a reality. Moreover, in his opinion, it is a useless hypothesis, for everyone admits that it is sometimes possible to have ideas without corporeal substance, this being proved by what happens in dreams, deliriums, etc. Now if this hypothesis is not necessary to explain the existence of our ideas upon certain occasions, what reason is there for considering it necessary upon all other occasions? What is more, those who support the hypothesis admit that they cannot understand how material substance can act upon the mind or how it is possible for the former to leave the imprint

3. *Ibid.*, sec. 18.

of an idea upon the latter.[4] Berkeley concludes that if there were corporeal substances it would be impossible for us to know them and if there were none we should have the same reasons for believing that they do exist as we have now.[5]

Berkeley's position with regard to corporeal substance was subject to hasty ridicule by those who did not fully realize its philosophical meaning. It was believed possible, for example, to refute it by stating that it is ridiculous to maintain that when we sit upon a chair we are merely sitting upon our own perceptions.[6] It was to answer such objections as these that Berkeley had taken special pains to point out that he denied not the existence of objects but a doctrine designed to interpret matter. "I do not argue against the existence of any one thing that we can apprehend, either by sense or reflection. That the things I see with my eyes and touch with my hands do exist, really exist, I make not the least question. The only thing whose existence we deny is that which *philosophers* call Matter or corporeal substance." [7] Berkeley goes further and maintains that the everyday view is in agreement with his thesis, for what he understands as meant by matter is the "*combination* of sensible qualities." [8] His philosophy, therefore, eliminates not natural objects but merely a false

4. *Ibid.*, sec. 19 .
5. *Ibid.*, sec. 20.
6. The mistake in this type of attack lies in considering the chair in its philosophical sense, according to Berkeley, and forgetting to consider our bodies in the same way.
7. *Principles*, sec. 35.
8. *Ibid.*, sec. 37.

philosophic doctrine—the notion of corporeal substance.

The technique of this elimination of material substance is quite obvious. One destroys the unity of objects and demonstrates that they are no more than the sum of their qualities, for the empirical method does not admit as reality what cannot be observed. Substance, in the traditional sense, cannot be observed and is therefore reduced to the status of a useless hypothesis and tossed upon the junk pile.

Berkeley feels no need to explain the integration of the qualities which constitute an object, which is what forces Locke to posit a substance to support these qualities; he simply states that objects are constituted by the *combination* of their sensible qualities.

In this long discursive process which begins as a thoroughgoing criticism of the doctrine of general abstract ideas and ends with the rejection of matter, it is easy to observe how the idea of substance disintegrates in Berkeley's hands as it passes from an unknown but necessary presupposition in Locke to an unnecessary, contradictory, and absurd hypothesis in Berkeley.

4. Spiritual substance and the conflict of the two criteria

Up to this point we have considered substance only in its material aspect.

Does Berkeley apply the same method to the analysis of the thinking substance? Does he also reject the self as a mere abstract idea, since nothing is left if we deprive it of its "operations"? In other words, what idea, in

Berkeley's sense, can we form of a self if we take away
its perceptions, desires, resolutions, doubts, joys, and an-
gers—in a word, its "thoughts"?

Berkeley conceived of a "concrete logic" which led him
to a psychological empiricism that eliminated everything
that could not be conceived of, represented. But he aban-
dons this concrete logic when he considers the res
cogitans. As in the case of Locke, there arises a struggle
here between the new ideas and the old prejudices. The
new ideas penetrate and destroy some of the old prejudices
but are arrested when they come up against others that
are still overpoweringly strong. In Berkeley's case the
situation may be explained not only by historical reasons
but also by personal ones. A man of his religious voca-
tion, who eventually became bishop of Cloyne, could not
afford to reach the conclusions, with regard to things of
the spirit, toward which his method was leading him.
Thus the res cogitans had to wait for Hume from whom
it suffers the same fate which the res extensa received at
the hands of Bishop Berkeley.

Let us first examine Berkeley's position with regard to
the res cogitans and try to see if it is immune, on the
spiritual level, to the same type of objections that he himself raised on the level of material substance.

Berkeley passes from the criticism of corporeal substance to the affirmation of the existence of the spirit
in a way which clearly shows the connection between his
immaterialism and his spiritualism but which leaves room
for many doubts concerning the legitimacy of his reasoning. As a matter of fact, once he has proved the existence

of ideas he investigates the cause "whereon they depend, and which produces and changes them"; [9] this cannot be another idea, for ideas are inactive—"There is nothing of power or agency included in them." [1] If one idea cannot occasion any alteration in another idea, the cause of ideas and their changes, states Berkeley, must be a substance. "But it has been shewn that there is no corporeal or material substance: it remains therefore that the cause of ideas is an incorporeal active substance or Spirit." [2]

It is a very uncritical conception of causality, perhaps inspired by Locke,[3] which permits Berkeley to reintroduce the idea of substance, though it is now restricted to the spiritual realm. Berkeley understands by spirit, mind, or soul "that indivisible, unextended thing which thinks, acts and perceives," [4] or, according to another passage, "A Spirit is one simple, undivided, active being—as it perceives ideas it is called the *understanding*, and as it produces or otherwise operates about them it is called the *will*." [5]

Berkeley declares that the terms spirit, soul, self, and spiritual substance are synonymous.[6] That he interprets the self in a substantial sense is seen not only in his use of the term and in the context of his doctrine but also in his explicit statement that the spirit is "the only substance

9. *Ibid.*, sec. 26.
1. *Ibid.*, sec. 25.
2. *Ibid.*, sec. 26.
3. Cf. *Essay*, II, 21; IV, 10.
4. *Dialogues*, III, ed. Fraser, 1, 448.
5. *Principles*, sec. 27.
6. *Ibid.*, sec. 139.

or support wherein unthinking beings or ideas can exist." [7] His interpretation of substance as the support of ideas, operations, or qualities sets in sharp contrast his conception of the self and the critical attitude that he had adopted with regard to material substance and abstract ideas. As a matter of fact, how can we accept his statement that spiritual substance *supports* ideas when he has written, referring satirically to corporeal substance, that he is at a loss to explain what meaning can be derived from the statement that substance *supports* accidents? [8]

Is not spirit just one more abstract idea? It is evident that we cannot form an idea of spirit, in the Berkeleian sense of the term. He himself recognizes this. We cannot by means of ideas, which are passive and inert,[9] frame a representation of spirit, whose chief characteristic is its activity.[1] But, though Berkeley rejects the theory that we have an *idea* of spirit, he concedes that we have a *notion* of it, "that is, we understand the meaning of the word, otherwise we could not affirm or deny anything of it." [2] Why could not the same criterion be applied to

7. *Ibid.*, sec. 135. In sec. 141 he calls it "an active, simple, uncompounded substance."

8. *Ibid.*, secs. 16, 17.

9. *Ibid.*, sec. 25.

1. *Ibid.*, sec. 137: "That an *idea*, which is inactive, and the existence whereof consists in being perceived, should be the image or likeness of an agent subsisting by itself, seems to need no other refutation than barely attending to what is meant by those words."

2. *Ibid.*, sec. 140. In sec. 142 he writes: "I have some knowledge or notion of *my mind*, and its acts about ideas; inasmuch

corporeal substance? If it is not possible to have an idea of matter, at least we could have a notion of it, for otherwise "we could not affirm or deny anything of it."

I am not, of course, defending the existence of corporeal substance. What I wish to make clear is the incompatibility of the criteria by which Berkeley judges corporeal and spiritual substances. To what may we attribute this duality in criteria? It may obviously be attributed to the theological considerations motivating him: he wished to prove the "natural immortality of the soul" [3] and the "existence and immateriality of God." If he had applied to the res cogitans his theory concerning abstract ideas, as set forth in the introduction to his *Principles*, or concerning corporeal substance, as seen in the first 25 sections, Berkeley would have been obliged to adopt an attitude similar to that of Hume. This would have been difficult to reconcile with his religious convictions. It is not, then, a matter of difficulty on the purely theoretical plane but a matter of a conflict between his "new principles" and a religious conviction just as strong and sincere as those principles.

The existence of this inner conflict is better seen if one casts a glance at Berkeley's philosophical growth and at the period in which he discovered his "first principles." The *Commonplace Book* is an important source for the study of this period.[4] It reveals that, at the beginning,

---

as I know or understand what is meant by these words. What I know, that I have some notion of."

3. *Ibid.*, sec. 141.

4. One must, of course, make clear whether one is considering

Berkeley had conceived of the self in accordance with and not in conflict with his logic and his empirical attitude. He writes, for example, "Take away perceptions and you take away the mind. Put the perceptions and you put the mind"; [5] this shows not only the importance of the states or perceptions that constitute the spirit or mind but also the absence of a substantial being beneath these states.[6] On the same note, Berkeley actually anticipates, in almost the very same words, Hume's thesis concerning the self—"Mind is a congeries of perceptions." [7] And what is more, he assumes a skeptical attitude with regard to the intuitive apprehension of the self.[8]

Even in the *Principles* one runs across certain passages that run counter to substantialism, when Berkeley is lay-

---

Bk. A or B, especially since some writers have maintained that Bk. A was written in 1715 or 1716, that is, when Berkeley had abandoned the attitude which he defends in the *Principles*.

5. *Commonplace Book*, ed. Johnston, No. 586.

6. At the end of the *Commonplace Book* he wrote: "Pure intellect I understand not." Ed. Johnston, No. 822.

7. *Ibid.*, No. 586. As will be recalled, Hume's words were, "a bundle or collection of different perceptions." *Treatise of Human Nature*, Bk. I, Pt. IV, sec. vi.

G. Dawes Hicks believes that in this note Berkeley merely wished to state that the spirit cannot exist without ideas. Cf. his *Berkeley* (Oxford, Oxford University Press, 1932), p. 150. John Wild maintains that the meaning which I propose can be attributed to this passage only if it is isolated from its context. Cf. his study, *George Berkeley, a Study of His Life and Philosophy* (Cambridge, Mass., 1936), pp. 41-2.

8. *Commonplace Book*, ed. Johnston, No. 239.

ing more emphasis on the attribute and so slights substance. As we know, he admits the existence of only two kinds of beings—ideas and spirits. The existence of an idea consists in being perceived.[9] In what does the existence of a spirit consist? It consists in knowing, in perceiving ideas, and in exercising "divers operations, as willing, imagining, remembering, about them." [1] This activistic conception of spirit [2] obliges Berkeley to defend Descartes against Locke and to maintain that it is "a plain consequence that the soul always thinks" and that it is "no easy task" [3] to abstract its existence from its thinking. The dependence of the self upon its activity is extremely great (see below, nn. 2 and 3) . He writes in the *Commonplace Book:* "Certainly if there were no sensible ideas there could be no soul, no perception, remembrance, love, fear, & c.; no faculty could be exerted." [4]

9. *Principles*, sec. 2.

1. *Ibid.* The active nature of the spirit may be seen even more clearly in sec. 139. Cf. *Commonplace Book*, Nos. 586, 623.

2. In the *Commonplace Book* he writes: "The Will is *purus actus*, or rather pure spirit, not imaginable, not sensible, not intelligible, in no wise the object of the understanding, no wise perceivable" (No. 840). Cf. No. 718. In another note (No. 860) he writes, "I must include understanding and will & c. in the word Spirit—by which I mean all that is active."

3. *Principles*, sec. 98. In the *Commonplace Book* he wrote: "The mind always and constantly thinks" (No. 660). In this case, however, he is not referring to a finite mind but to the Spirit. Farther on he notes, "To say the mind exists without thinking is a contradiction, nonsense, nothing" (No. 661).

4. *Commonplace Book*, No. 479.

What remains if we take away from the spirit its process of thought? One might answer, "substance," though it must be deprived of existence since it has been separated from its essential attribute, i.e. thought. Berkeley does not answer the question in this way, however; he does not even confront the problem, perhaps because confronting it would have forced him to see that he was facing a situation similar to the one concerning corporeal substance. If we eliminate the qualities of a body—its extension, form, weight, color, etc.—nothing remains, he says. This is not because substance cannot exist without its attributes but because there *is* no "substance": the body is a *combination* of its qualities, and a hypostasis of substance simply means the postulation of an unknown and evanescent something that supports these qualities. Now are we not facing the same situation with regard to spirit? Why not maintain that the spirit, too, is merely a combination of its *cogitationes* since its existence depends upon thinking and disappears as soon as thought is eliminated? And if one wishes to state the problem on the epistemological level—as Berkeley does with regard to the res extensa— how do we know the thinking substance? We do not know extended substance but rather extension and other qualities; does not the same thing happen in the case of spirit? "We cannot know the existence of *other spirits* otherwise than by their operations." [5] Why are we to suppose that there is a substance that supports these operations? Why do we not take them as they are presented to us, which is what we did with the qualities of bodies? The

5. *Principles*, sec. 145.

reference to "other spirits" [6] and the mediate character of our knowledge of another person seems to imply that we know something more than operations in the case of our own self. Berkeley states that we know our own self "immediately or intuitively" [7] but does not expressly say that intuition reveals to us its substantial character. It is understood that the knowledge of our own cogitationes may be immediate and intuitive, but exactly at what point or in what way do we become aware of the supposed substance or support of these cogitationes? In the ten sections which Berkeley devotes particularly to the study of spirit in his *Principles*,[8] or even in the rest of the book and all the rest of his writings, we find no answer to this question. The only things that we find are the statement already quoted, that "spirit is the only substance or support wherein . . . ideas can exist," and long wearisome explanations, which we have already partially examined, as to why we cannot have an *idea* of spirit though we do have a *notion* of it. What does it mean, that I have a notion of my spirit? It means, according to Berkeley, that "I know or understand what is meant by these words." [9] Very well; but perhaps I understand by these words the sum of my cogitationes. Let us repeat our question in a more concrete form: At what point and in what way do we conceive a *notion* of the substantial aspect of our own spirit? One seeks in vain to find a reply to this or an explanation of it; the substantialist presupposition makes

6. *Ibid.*
7. *Dialogues*, III, ed. Fraser, 1, 447–8.
8. I.e. *Principles*, secs. 135–44.
9. *Ibid.*, sec. 142.

its appearance again. With respect to thinking substance, Berkeley adopts the same attitude which Descartes and Locke adopted with respect to extended substance and which so irritated Berkeley himself—substance *must* exist because of the fact that we cannot think of any way in which the attributes or qualities could possibly exist per se. In other words, we have the old argument that it is "self-evident"; this may make sense in the case of a rationalist, but it is in radical contradiction to Berkeley's empirical principles. What is more, whenever he is not dogmatically affirming the substantial nature of spirit but approaching an *explanation* of its nature or of the possibilities of knowing it, the empiricist in him seems to play traitor to the substantialist. In the important passage in which he defines spirit he adds that "such is the nature of Spirit, or that which acts, that it cannot be of itself perceived, but only by the effects which it produceth." [1] And farther on he maintains that "by the word *spirit* [2] we mean only that which thinks, wills, and perceives; this, and this alone, constitutes the signification of that term." [3] And he adds that because it is impossible to have an idea of such operations it is evident that we can have no idea of spirit.

How can we reconcile these passages with the supposed "immediate or intuitive" knowledge which, according to another passage, we have of the spirit? What is it that we know intuitively—the spirit in its totality, its

1. *Ibid.*, sec. 27.
2. "Spirit" here includes our own spirit.
3. *Principles*, sec. 138.

substantial character, or only its operations and effects?

Berkeley offers no solution for this intricate maze of difficulties and incompatible doctrines. In my opinion it is impossible to reconcile the criterion which he adopts with respect to matter with that which he then adopts with respect to spirit. Let us analyze one final case in which, once again, the contradiction is obvious. Berkeley writes:

> As to what philosophers say of subject and mode, that seems very groundless and unintelligible. For instance, in this proposition "a die is hard, extended, and square," they will have it that the word *die* denotes a subject or substance, distinct from the hardness, extension, and figure which are predicated of it, and in which they exist. This I cannot comprehend: to me a die seems to be nothing distinct from those things which are termed its modes or accidents. And, to say a die is hard, extended, and square is not to attribute those qualities to a subject distinct from and supporting them, but only an explication of the meaning of the word *die*.[4]

But when he refers to spirit he characterizes it as a "perceiving, acting being"[5] and interprets this being as "spiritual substance." Why does he maintain that when we state that a die is hard, extended, and square we are not attributing qualities to a substance but only explaining the meaning of the word "die" and then make an

4. *Ibid.*, sec. 49.
5. *Ibid.*, sec. 2.

about-face and maintain that if we characterize the spirit as that which desires, perceives, etc. we are not explaining the word "spirit"?

As in the case of Locke, it is easy to discover Berkeley's real contribution, even though it is sometimes hidden by a tangle of contradictions and non sequiturs. I refer to his contribution to the development of modern thought, that is, to the ideas that have had more influence upon subsequent thinkers. His main contribution seems to be limited to his criticism of general abstract ideas and his empirical analysis of the conception of material substance. His spiritualism and theism, on the other hand, had less influence upon later thought.

Although we must reject the interpretation of certain historians, who consider the various philosophers as mere steps or stages in a process which leads up to their own conception or to that of a classic philosopher which they choose as the final word in philosophy, we must not make the mistake of going to the opposite extreme and maintaining that each thinker is a "windowless monad," an island completely cut off from all communication by a vast empty sea. Each philosopher works on the problems of his own particular age, and even the most revolutionary ones would make no sense at all if they ignored all thought that had preceded them. Hence the history of philosophy has a certain sense of direction, even though there be no concrete goal, and in some periods it is easy to note the general direction in which ideas are developing. Such is the case with the period which extends from Locke to Hume. One is therefore obliged to judge Berkeley's personality and contribution in the light of the leading ideas of the process in which he was involved, that is, the process of the dissolution of the substantialist *Weltanschauung*. It may, in brief, be summed up thus: Locke, completely conditioned by substantialism, interprets substance as that which supports qualities, and when he studies substance for the first time in the light of an empirical method he recognizes its obscure origin and unknowable nature. Thus Berkeley receives from Locke the idea of substance as an empty "I-know-not-what" and, using Locke's conceptual equipment, has no difficulty in dispensing with it altogether on the material level. However, he retains spiritual substance due to metaphysical and theological influences. Hume, having no such reasons, applies to the spirit the same method which his predecessor had applied to matter, and the modern substantialist view, which began with Descartes, came to the end of the great cycle of dissolution. Such is Berkeley's position in the historical process which we are studying. Let us now examine in detail Hume's contribution.

CHAPTER IV

Hume's Analysis of Substance and Personal Identity

1. Hume's empiricism

One is impressed by the great clarity with which Hume presents his ideas. The one thing that he could never be criticized for is that his doctrine suffers from obscurity or that his system is confused. His characteristic critical spirit and ability to convince derive from the simplicity and clarity of his ideas. In the light of his principles old problems seem to vanish, and philosophic discourse acquires a luminosity and consistency which it had never had before. But the clarity and coherence of his ideas do not, of course, prove anything concerning their legitimacy as a description of reality. There are systems that are clear and coherent, yet false.

His basic point of departure is similar to that of Locke. Hume maintains, at the beginning of his *Treatise of Human Nature*, that in man's mind there are only "impressions" and "ideas." These two elements constitute the whole of the mind's content and are what Hume calls "perceptions," a term which is equivalent to Locke's "ideas" and which Hume took from Francis Hutcheson.[1] The difference between impressions and ideas depends upon the degrees of force and vivacity with which they present themselves to our mind and make a way for themselves into our thought and consciousness: impressions penetrate with more force and violence, while ideas are but the weak images of impressions.[2] For Hume, impressions include sensations as well as passions and emotions, when for the first time they present themselves to the mind. Hume believes that he is "restoring the word, idea, to its original sense, from which Mr. Locke had perverted it" [3] and explains that the term "impression" does not express "the manner, in which our lively perceptions are produced in the soul, but merely the perceptions themselves; for which there is no particular name in the English or any other language that I know of." [4] It seems that here Hume is not trying to distinguish between the act of perception and the thing perceived; he is, rather, insisting

1. Hutcheson influenced Hume in many different ways, as was demonstrated by Norman Kemp Smith in his acute study of the origin of Hume's philosophy, *The Philosophy of David Hume. A Critical Study of Its Origins and Central Doctrines* (London, Macmillan, 1941). Cf. especially Pt. I, chaps. i, ii.

2. Hume repeats these ideas, which are fundamental to his philosophy, in his *Enquiry Concerning Human Understanding*, sec. 2.

3. A *Treatise of Human Nature*, Bk. I, Pt. i, sec. 1 (1, 312 n. 1, in the edition from which we shall quote, that of T. H. Green and T. H. Grose [London, Longmans, Green, 1890]).

4. *Ibid.* Montaigne and Malebranche had already used the term "impression"; Hume is the first to use it in English.

on his belief that one must consider impressions just as they are presented and not as images of something that transcends them. This is true even in the case of sensations but is obvious in the case of emotions and passions. For what could the emotions and passions be copies of?

Both impressions and ideas can be simple or complex. They are simple if they do not admit of distinction or separation; they are complex, on the other hand, if they can be divided into parts. Though many of our complex ideas have no corresponding impressions and though our complex impressions are not always copied with precision by our ideas, the relation between impressions and simple ideas admits of no exceptions: every simple idea has a simple impression that resembles it, and every simple impression has a corresponding idea. This permits Hume to establish the central principle of his philosophy: *"That all our simple ideas in their first appearance, are derived from simple impressions, which are correspondent to them, and which they exactly represent."* [5]

According to Hume, anyone can prove the truth of this statement by examining himself; and whoever would try to disprove it must find a simple idea which has no corresponding impression or a simple impression which does not give rise to a corresponding idea.

Every idea rests upon an impression; impressions always precede ideas. Even among impressions there is a certain priority; of the two kinds of impressions—sensations and reflections—the former kind "arises in the soul

5. *Ibid.*, I, i, 1 (1, 314).

originally, from unknown causes," [6] and the latter is derived from our ideas. The following is Hume's explanation of the process which gives rise to the "impressions of reflexion," i.e. passions, desires, and emotions. An impression arouses the senses and causes us to perceive heat or coldness, pleasure or pain. The mind retains a copy after the impression has ceased. This copy is what Hume calls "idea." When this idea of pleasure or pain again arises in the mind it produces new impressions of desire, hope, and fear, which can be called impressions of reflection since they derive from reflection. These, in turn, become ideas when copied by the memory and the imagination and can, in turn, give rise to other impressions and ideas. The impressions of reflection, hence, are prior to the corresponding ideas but are subsequent to the "impressions of sensation" from which they derive.

But if every legitimate idea must be able to reflect the impression that has given rise to it,

> When we entertain, therefore, any suspicion that a philosophical term is employed without any meaning or idea (as is but too frequent), we need but enquire, *from what impression is that supposed idea derived?* And if it be impossible to assign any, this will serve to confirm our suspicion. By bringing ideas into so clear a light we may reasonably hope to remove all dispute, which may arise concerning their nature and reality.[7]

6. *Ibid.*, I, i, 2 (1, 317).
7. *Enquiry*, sec. 2, *in fine*.

2. *His idea of substance*

Within the framework given in the preceding paragraphs Hume sets about the task of examining the idea of substance. It is easy to foresee the result. In the first part of Book I of the *Treatise* Hume maintains that if the idea of substance is legitimate it must derive from an impression, whether of sensation or reflection, for such impressions, as we have seen, are the two sole legitimate sources of ideas. Now then, if it derives from a sensible impression, through which sense does the impression reach us? If it is the sense of vision, substance must be a color; if it is the sense of hearing, it is a sound, etc. Eliminating in this way the possibility that it derive from a sensible impression, we still have the possibility that it derives from an impression of reflection. But it is easy to see that this route too is cut off, for impressions of reflection give rise to passions, emotions, etc., which cannot represent substance since they have reference to particular states or qualities.[8] Hume confirms this line of reasoning at the end of the first book when he writes:

> As every idea is derived from a precedent impression, had we any idea of the substance of our minds, we must also have an impression of it; which is very difficult, if not impossible, to be conceived. For how can an impression represent a substance, otherwise than by resembling it? And how can an impression resemble a substance, since, according to this philos-

8. Cf. *Treatise*, I, i, 6.

ophy, it is not a substance, and has none of the peculiar qualities or characteristics of a substance? [9]

Hume applied to substance, whether material or spiritual, the same method that Berkeley used in order to get rid of material substance alone. He seems to realize this, for he writes in the appendix: "Philosophers begin to be reconciled to the principle, *that we have no idea of external substance, distinct from the ideas of particular qualities.* This must pave the way for a like principle with regard to the mind, *that we have no notion of it, distinct from the particular perception.*" [1]

As an empiricist, Hume could not deny that we have an idea of substance. What he did reject was the conception that "metaphysicians" had of substance, and he proposed instead an explanation concerning the origin and nature of this idea. To what metaphysicians was Hume referring? Which of the two conceptions of substance then prevalent—res per se subsistens and substans accidentibus—did he have in mind?

In the section which he devotes to "the immateriality of the soul" [2] there are important passages which, despite the fact that they complement and clarify the ideas set forth in the often quoted brief section concerning "modes and substances," [3] have seldom been commented upon by those who have attempted to analyze the conception

9. *Ibid.,* I, iv, 5 (1, 517).
1. *Ibid.,* 1, 559.
2. *Ibid.,* I, iv, 5.
3. *Ibid.,* I, i, 6.

of substance in Hume. These passages reveal to us what sort of substance he had in mind in his criticism of it. As a matter of fact, although there is a brief reference to substance as "something which may exist by itself," [4] in his whole study of the problem he has in mind a conception of substance as a substratum which *supports* different modifications without itself undergoing any alteration. The doctrine which Hume rejects is that of those philosophers who conceived of substance as something "in which they suppose our perceptions to inhere." [5] And he proceeds to ask, "*What [do] they mean by substance and inhesion?*" [6] In the section devoted to substance he speaks of "an unknown *something*, in which they [the particular qualities] are supposed to inhere." [7] That Hume's attack is directed against the conception of substance as a substans accidentibus is even more clearly apparent in the passage in which he gives an exposition of the doctrine of substance of Spinoza who, as it is well known, considered it as "that which is in itself and is conceived through itself." Hume writes:

> Every passion of the soul; every configuration of matter, however different and various, inhere in the same substance, and preserve in themselves their characters of distinction, without communicating them to that subject, in which they inhere. The same *substratum*, if I may so speak, supports the

4. *Ibid.*, I, iv, 5 (1, 517).
5. *Ibid.*
6. *Ibid.*
7. *Ibid.*, I, i, 6 (1, 324).

most different modifications, without any difference in itself; and varies them, without any variation. Neither time, nor place, nor all the diversity of nature are able to produce any composition or change in its perfect simplicity and identity.[8]

Such is the doctrine of substance which Hume rejects. He does not, as is generally affirmed, discard the idea of substance but discards merely the interpretation of this idea which "certain philosophers" give. As Norman Kemp Smith correctly observes,[9] it can be stated in general terms that Hume never denies the existence of something that has been the object of controversy. The task he sets himself is that of freeing the idea under discussion from misunderstandings and inadequate interpretations in order to restore to it its legitimate meaning. This is the reason that he adds to his critique an explanation concerning the nature of the idea of substance. It is as follows: If every idea derives from an impression and if it is impossible to have impressions of anything but particular qualities, substance is then nothing more than a "collection of particular qualities," [1] a "collection of simple ideas." [2] What is it that causes particular qualities thus to constitute a "collection"? What, or who, unites the simple ideas that constitute a substance? The imagination, answers Hume. Substances are nothing more than

8. *Ibid.*, I, iv, 5 (1, 524).
9. Smith, *The Philosophy of David Hume*, p. 254.
1. *Treatise*, I, i, 6 (1, 324).
2. *Ibid.*

collections of simple ideas to which imagination gives unity and we give definite names so as to be able to call the object to mind (be it our own mind or that of another person).

According to Hume, there is no intrinsic reason for bringing together the qualities which constitute a determined substance. Thus, for example, the idea which we have of gold can at first include the simple ideas of yellow color, weight, malleability, fusibility. But when we subsequently discover that gold is soluble in *aqua regia* we add to the other qualities that of solubility and from then on suppose that it belongs to the substance which we call gold just as though solubility, from the beginning, had formed part of that compound idea which we designate by the word "gold." [3] In the same way we can take away some of its qualities without losing the idea of the substance of gold. The only important matter is that there should be maintained in our imaginations the relation of continuity and causation.

The same thing does not happen in the case of modes. Modes are formed of simple ideas in which there is not sufficient relation of continuity and causation for us to consider them as real things. Or they may represent scattered qualities in different subjects. They are not produced arbitrarily, and Hume devotes little space to them because the philosophers have not abused them—as they have abused substances—and consequently have not given rise to serious errors or confusions.

Hume kept the same central conception of substance

3. *Ibid.*

for many years after the publication of his *Treatise*. In a letter dated 1746 he writes to Henry Home that "As to the idea of substance, I must own, that as it has no access to the mind by any of our senses or feelings, it has always appeared to me to be nothing but our imaginary centre of union amongst the different and variable qualities that are to be found in every piece of matter." [4]

As T. H. Green correctly points out,[5] Hume's explanation of the idea of substance is identical to Locke's, with this modification: Hume eliminates the positing of an unknowable substratum, which the author of the *Essay* had timidly upheld. Locke writes:

The mind being, as I have declared, furnished with a great number of the simple ideas, conveyed in by the senses as they are found in exterior things, or by reflection on its own operations, takes notice also that a certain number of these simple ideas go constantly together; which being presumed to belong to one thing, and words being suited to common apprehensions, and made use of for quick dispatch, are called, so united in one subject, by one name; which, by inadvertency, we are apt afterward to talk of and consider as one simple idea, which indeed is a complication of many ideas together: because, as I have said, not imagining how these simple ideas *can* subsist by themselves, we accustom ourselves to

4. See *The Letters of David Hume*, ed. J. Y. T. Greig (Oxford, Clarendon Press, 1932), 1, 94.
5. Cf. introduction to A *Treatise of Human Nature*, 1, 177.

suppose some *substratum* wherein they do subsist, and from which they do result, which therefore we call *substance*.[6]

3. *Personal identity*

The method which Hume uses to get rid of the usual conception of personal identity is similar to that which he applied to the idea of substance. At the beginning of section 6 of the *Treatise*, he puts this question: Since, as we have seen, every legitimate idea must derive from an impression, from what impression does the idea of the self derive? He notes at once the impossibility of answering this question without falling into an obvious and absurd self-contradiction, for the self cannot be an impression if it is that to which many of our impressions and ideas are referred. He insists, nevertheless, that the question must be answered if we really do hope to have a "clear and intelligible" idea of the self. Although it is very well known, the passage in which he gives us an account of his fruitless search for the self is worth rereading:

> For my part, when I enter most intimately into what I call *myself*, I always stumble on some particular perception or other, of heat or cold, light or shade, love or hatred, pain or pleasure. I never can catch *myself* at any time without a perception, and never can observe any thing but the perception. When my perceptions are removed for any time, as by sound sleep; so long am I insensible of *myself*, and may

6. *Essay*, II, xxiii, 1.

truly be said not to exist. And were all my perceptions removed by death, and could I neither think,
nor feel, nor see, nor love, nor hate after the dissolution of my body, I should be entirely annihilated,
nor do I conceive what is farther requisite to make
me a perfect non-entity.[7]

When one has recovered from the impression of strong
conviction in this passage, it occurs to one to ask what it
is that Hume did not find. Or, in other words, what was
he seeking? The answer cannot be merely, "the self," for
there are many possible types of self which Hume's
analysis could not eliminate. The general context and the
passages which precede and follow what has been quoted
clearly reveal that what Hume was looking for was a simple, independent, immutable self, that is to say, a substantial self.

The first attribute, simplicity, is explicitly acknowledged; the other two are implicit at various points in
the course of his analysis. He writes that someone else
"may, perhaps, perceive something *simple* and continued,
which he calls *himself*; though I am certain there is no
such principle in me." [8]

The idea of the independence of the self with respect
to perceptions may be found in the passage cited above,
which reads: "And were all my perceptions removed by
death, and could I neither think, nor feel, nor see, nor
love, nor hate after the dissolution of my body, I should

7. *Treatise*, I, iv, 6 (1, 534).
8. *Ibid.*, I, iv, 6 (1, 534). Italics mine.

be entirely annihilated, nor do I conceive what is farther requisite to make me a perfect non-entity." [9] Similarly, in the appendix he writes that the perceptions "must be the same with self; since the one cannot survive the other." [1] The substantialist presuppositions which still lingered in his mind kept him from seeing that independence is not the essential attribute of whatever exists and that the temporary or permanent suppression of "perceptions" may bring as a consequence the suppression of the self without the former necessarily being the same thing as the latter. It never occurred to him that "perceptions" and the self could be indissolubly united, to such an extent that both must suffer the same fate.

The conception of the self as an immutable being is expressed with even greater clarity. "If any impression gives rise to the idea of self, that impression must continue *invariably the same*, through the whole course of our lives; since self is supposed to exist after that manner. But there is no impression *constant and invariable*." [2] Why should one suppose that the self is immutable? Why cannot we accept the possibility of a changing self, in the same way that we can accept the existence of a self that depends upon "perceptions"?

An examination of the passage in the appendix in which he once more brings up the matter of the self confirms the above-indicated interpretation. Not only does he repeat many times, as we have noticed, the idea of the

9. *Ibid.*, 1, 534.
1. *Ibid.*, 1, 559.
2. *Ibid.*, I, iv, 6 (1, 533). Italics mine.

supposedly simple and independent nature of the self, but he actually goes as far as to speak of the "self or substance" and then to ask if self is the same thing as substance. If self is the same thing as substance, he adds, "how can that question have place, concerning the subsistence of self, under a change of substance? If they be distinct, what is the difference betwixt them?" [3] And he notes that he himself has no notion of either one, when they are conceived of as distinct from particular perceptions.

That Hume has in mind a substantial self is confirmed by many other passages in the *Treatise*. Upon referring to the mind in a passage which precedes those which we have examined, he states that it is "supposed, though falsely, to be endowed with a perfect simplicity and identity." [4] Farther on he rejects the self because "There is properly no *simplicity* in it at one time, nor *identity* in different . . ." [5] In the section devoted to the "immateriality of the soul," he speaks in turn of the idea which we may have of "the substance of our mind" [6] and examines *in extenso* the substantialist conception of the soul.

But this does not end the matter. The substantialist vein of thought, which he has been criticizing, seems to crop out again when he transfers to the "perceptions" those characteristics of substance which he did not find in

3. *Ibid.*, 1, 559.
4. *Ibid.*, I, iv, 2 (1, 495).
5. *Ibid.*, I, iv, 6 (1, 534). Hume's italics.
6. *Ibid.*, I, iv, 5 (1, 517).

the self. As a matter of fact when, for the second time in the *Treatise*, he takes up the idea of substance and the possibility that it may be defined as "something that exists *per se*," Hume reasons in the following way:

> Whatever is clearly conceived may exist; and whatever is clearly conceived, after any manner, may exist after the same manner. This is one principle, which has been already acknowledged. Again, every thing, which is different, is distinguishable, and every thing which is distinguishable, is separable by the imagination. This is another principle. My conclusion from both is, that since all our perceptions are different from each other, and from every thing else in the universe, they are also distinct and separable, and may be considered as separately existent, and may exist separately, and have no need of any thing else to support their existence. They are therefore substances, as far as this definition explains a substance.[7]

The foregoing consideration of Hume's critique of personal identity makes it possible for us to place the Scotch philosopher in the historical context to which he belongs and not to read into his words more than they actually contain. What he denies is the substantial self and not every form of the self, as some of his modern followers erroneously believe.

Just as Hume did not see fit to reject the idea of substance supported by the metaphysicians without propos-

7. *Ibid.*, I, iv, 5 (1, 518).

ing an explanation of its nature and origin, so also would he not see fit to deny the existence of the substantial self without offering us his views as to the way in which the self should be understood.

What is the self for Hume? The first answer that he gives us is the one which is usually accepted as his basic view—the self is nothing more than "a bundle or collection of different perceptions, which succeed each other with an inconceivable rapidity, and are in a perpetual flux and movement." [8] Or as he writes in an earlier passage, "The mind is nothing but a heap or collection of different perceptions." [9] In these instances Hume, perhaps as a reaction against the postulation of a metaphysical principle that assured the simplicity and identity of the self,[1] is going to the opposite extreme of maintaining that what really exist are the perceptions, which are differentiated *inter se* and can exist separately. Our eyes cannot turn in their sockets without changing our perceptions, and our thoughts are changing even more continually than our visual perceptions. Hume compares the mind to a theater "where several perceptions successively make their appearance; pass, re-pass, glide away, and mingle in an infinite variety of postures and situations." [2] But this comparison should not deceive us by leading us to believe that there exists something in which the appearance of the various perceptions takes place. In truth, "they are

8. *Ibid.*, I, iv, 6 (1, 534).
9. *Ibid.*, I, iv, 2 (1, 495).
1. *Ibid.*
2. *Ibid.*, I, iv, 6 (1, 534-5).

the successive perceptions only, that constitute the mind; nor have we the most distant notion of the place, where these scenes are represented, or of the materials of which it is composed." [3]

Hume does not ignore the fact, however, that men believe in the identity of their own persons. He undertakes to determine what the reason or cause for this belief may be. The explanation he gives for this belief has, by some of Hume's students, been confused with his own conceptions of personal identity. If one reads with care the famous section 6 of the *Treatise*, he will discover that the author makes a distinction between his own view of personal identity and the theory which he proposes as an explanation of the usual belief in this identity.

In his attempt to explain this belief, Hume begins by distinguishing personal identity which has reference to our thought or imagination from personal identity which has reference to our passions. And he makes it clear that he is concerned with the first. Since he thinks that there is an important analogy between supposed personal identity and the identity of plants and animals, he examines first the latter and then the former.

What does Hume mean by "identity"? He designates as identity the "idea of an object, that remains invariable and uninterrupted through a supposed variation of time." [4] "Diversity," on the other hand, is the idea of different objects that exist successively and are found to be intimately interrelated. Despite the distinction evident

3. *Ibid.*
4. *Ibid.*, I, iv, 6 (1, 535).

between these two ideas, Hume thinks that they are sometimes confused because of the fact that the act of imagination by which an object is considered to be invariable
and uninterrupted and that by which a succession of related objects is perceived both impinge upon the mind in
the same way and that no more intellectual effort is re-
quired in the second case than in the first. This similarity
is responsible for the appearance of identity when what
actually exist are only related objects. For this reason,
Hume tries to prove that whenever identity is attributed
to objects that are not invariable and uninterrupted it is
actually a case of a succession of events related by contiguity, similarity, or causality.[5] What is more, this tendency to confuse one thing with another is reinforced by
the erroneous introduction of some metaphysical principle which serves to tie objects to one another and to
prevent their interruption and change. In this way arose
the notions of "soul," "self," "substance," which, it is
thought, give unity to perceptions. And when the nature of these concepts cannot be made clear, it is decided
to postulate an unknown, mysterious principle which
secretly connects the different parts and in this way assures the identity of the object.

It is the imagination which attributes identity to objects which have undergone modifications and hence have
ceased to be what they were. Sometimes this apparent
identity is due to the fact that the change has been very
slight, at least in proportion to the whole, sometimes to
the fact that it has been a gradual change. In the latter

5. *Ibid.*, 1, 536-7.

case, the easy uninterrupted flow from one moment to another gives the mind the illusion of continuous perception, and this leads to the postulation of the object's identity. It may be easily observed how the imagination postulates a nonexistent identity if one examines the case of plants and animals. Despite the fact that a plant or an animal, with the passage of time, undergoes a total change in the parts which constitute it and a change in form and size, we nevertheless attribute to it a supposed identity. This is due to the fact that we focus our attention upon the cooperation and common fate of the parts which constitute the plant or animal and that we suppose that these different parts maintain inter se a reciprocal relation of cause and effect in all their actions and operations.

The identity which we attribute to the mind of man is, according to Hume, just as fictitious as that which we attribute to plants and animals. It is, moreover, a matter of the same sort of identity, and they both have their origin in an analogous activity of the imagination.[6] That the identity of the mind is a fictitious product of the imagination is proved, says Hume, by the following line of reasoning. It is obvious, to him, that each one of the perceptions that make up the mind is distinct and separable from all the other perceptions, whether they are simultaneous or successive. It is also evident that the identity that we attribute to the mind is not able to reduce the different perceptions to a single one or to cause them to lose their distinctive characteristics. If it is maintained that the different perceptions are found to be

6. *Ibid.*, 1, 540.

united by identity, it will have to be asked whether this relation of identity is something that really binds the perceptions together or something which merely associates their ideas in the imagination. In other words, it is a question of whether we observe a real bond between the different perceptions or only feel it. That the understanding does not observe any real connection between objects —not even the relation of cause and effect—Hume accepts as already proved. It must therefore be concluded that "identity is nothing really belonging to these different perceptions, and uniting them together; but is merely a quality, which we attribute to them, because of the union of their ideas in the imagination, when we reflect upon them." [7]

The relations of contiguity, resemblance, and causality are, for Hume, the only ones that can explain the union in the imagination which we think we see between the different perceptions. In the study of this particular problem he first discards contiguity in the belief that it has little or no influence in the formation of this bond. He begins, then, with resemblance. He notes the influence that resemblance exercises in our conception of the identity of the self, if one pays attention to memory. Memory is the faculty by which we cause images of past perceptions to stir in our minds. And since the images resemble their objects, the imagination moves easily from one term to another and is under the illusion that it is dealing with a single object. Without memory it would not be possible to see the similarity between the different perceptions at

7. *Ibid.*

different moments; this similarity allows us to consider them as our own and to arrange them chronologically. Hence Hume reaches the conclusion that memory, in this case, not only discovers identity but contributes toward producing it.

There is, however, no doubt that causality is the relation which contributes most to our belief in personal identity. Our impressions give rise to corresponding ideas, and these ideas in turn produce new impressions. The perceptions are presented, then, united in a causal chain, and it is the causal relation which establishes the connection between the different changing parts which constitute the self. Hume thinks that an attentive examination of the passions corroborates what has been observed with regard to the imagination, since our distant perceptions influence one another mutually and cause us a "present concern" with our past or future pleasures and pains. It is memory, in turn, which discovers personal identity by showing the relation of cause and effect between the different perceptions. If we had no memory, we could not have acquired the notion of causality and consequently would have no idea of the causal chain which constitutes the self. But once we have acquired the notion of causality through memory we can extend the causal chain and, by the same token, the identity of our persons far beyond our memory. To those who maintain that it is memory alone which produces personal identity, Hume puts this question: How is it then possible that our personal identity can extend beyond our memory?

It is, consequently, the notion of causality which gives rise to our idea of personal identity. As a matter of fact, Hume writes that "the true idea of the human mind, is to consider it as a system of different perceptions of different existences, which are linked together by the relation of cause and effect, and mutually produce, destroy, influence, and modify each other." [8] Immediately following this he compares the soul to a republic or commonwealth in which the different members are united by reciprocal ties of government and subordination and give rise to other persons who propagate the same republic.

Some time ago we saw that it is customary to state that Hume's conception of the self is that it is a mere bundle of perceptions. But here we find a view which seems quite different from that. Which of the two represents more justly Hume's philosophy? Charles W. Hendel, after reproducing the passage just quoted, asks how it is possible, in the face of "Hume's definite statement," to continue to attribute to Hume the theory of the self as a mere bundle of perceptions.[9] In his opinion, this description tells us only what we can *observe*, if we think that we can look upon mind directly as an *object* of perception. But Hume disagrees with the "metaphysicians" and claims that what they really discover is not what they believe. In the passage just quoted—according to Hendel —Hume offers what he considers to be the true picture

8. *Ibid.*, 1, 541–2.

9. Charles W. Hendel Jr., *Studies in the Philosophy of David Hume* (Princeton, Princeton University Press, 1925), p. 248 n. 12.

of the mind so that we can understand how we come to believe in the identity of our own persons.

It seems to me that there is no such conflict between the two views presented by Hume. The theory of the self as a bundle of perceptions is, in my opinion, the better representation of Hume's conception. The other theory is not a new view of the self but *an explanation of the cause of our belief* in personal identity. For he recognizes, as an empiricist, that man believes in personal identity, and he observes that it is necessary to seek for the origin and cause of this belief. I base this interpretation upon the context which Hume establishes, after characterizing the self as a bundle of perceptions, by asking this question: "What then gives us so great a propension to *ascribe* an identity to these successive perceptions, and to *suppose* ourselves possessed of an invariable and uninterrupted existence through the whole course of our lives?" [1] In my opinion, everything that follows—including, of course, the definition to which note 8, page 99 refers—has one end in view: "to answer this question." [2] It should not be overlooked that farther on Hume writes: "The identity which we ascribe to the mind of man is only a fictitious one, and of a like kind with that which we ascribe to vegetables and animal bodies." [3] The so-called definition of the mind that we have been discussing forms part of the explanation of the fictitious "identity which we ascribe to the mind."

1. *Treatise*, I, iv, 6 (1, 535). Italics mine.
2. *Ibid*.
3. *Ibid*., 1, 540.

In the face of this quotation and the analysis which precedes it, it seems to be a waste of time to ask whether Hume denies personal identity, in the sense in which he defines it. It is not, however, equally vain to raise the question of Hume's final attitude with regard to the existence of a continuing self. Norman Kemp Smith maintains, in his excellent study of Hume, that he does not deny the existence of a continuing self.[4] This statement, too, seems to be based upon a confusion of Hume's theory of the self with his explanation of the reason for our belief in an identical, continuing self. The interpretations which Norman K. Smith proposes for the concepts of "fiction" and "fictitious"[5] do not alter Hume's basic view that "they are the successive perceptions only, that constitute the mind."[6] According to him, perceptions are all "different, and distinguishable, and separable from each other, and may be separately considered, and may exist separately, and have no need of any thing to support their existence."[7]

The proof that Hume denies the existence of a continuing self is to be sought not only in the familiar section 6 of the *Treatise*, which we have been concentrating upon, but also in the attitude which he assumes in the appendix.[8] Let us now turn our attention to that.

4. Cf. Smith, *Philosophy of David Hume*, pp. 96–9.
5. Cf. *ibid.*, pp. 96, 133–7.
6. *Treatise*, I, iv, 6 (1, 534).
7. *Ibid.*
8. The appendix was added to the end of the third volume of the *Treatise*, published in 1740; the first two volumes were pub-

4. The two principles which Hume
could not reconcile

Hume reveals in the appendix that he was aware of the limitations of his concept of the self. Again he denies the existence of a substantial self—simple, independent, and immutable—but he notes that along with the substantial substratum there also disappears the "principle of union" of which he speaks in his discussion of substance. Hence the self that remains is full of gaps which he would like to fill up but cannot.

Hume tells us in the appendix that there are two principles which he cannot reconcile, though he cannot renounce either one of them. Apparently the first principle is the result of his empirical and analytical attitude, and the second arises from his desire to give unity to that which he has knocked to pieces by applying the first principle. Here is the problem, as Hume presents it in the appendix. All perceptions are different from one another and therefore distinguishable and separable; they can exist and be conceived of separately, without the implication of any absurdity or contradiction. But if perceptions are different they can form a whole only if they are connected in some way. The human understanding, in turn, does not discover any connection between different existences, and "all my hopes vanish, when I come to ex-

lished together at the end of January 1739. Since Hume wrote the work in France in the years 1734–37, it is likely that he saw the difficulties in his theory of the self after his return to London in the fall of 1737.

plain the principles, that unite our successive perceptions in our thought or consciousness." [9]

Hume is unfortunate in his statement of the two incompatible principles. He writes: "In short there are two principles, which I cannot render consistent; nor is it in my power to renounce either of them, viz. *that all our distinct perceptions are distinct existences*, and *that the mind never perceives any real connexion among distinct existences.*" [1] I should say that the statement is unfortunate because these two principles are not incompatible; actually, the second is a consequence of the first. It is possible to conceive of a world in which everything is separate from everything else and in which the mind perceives no connection. There is no contradiction between these two characteristics of our imaginary world. The contradiction arises when one tries to reconcile this world with the principle of unity and connection. Such is Hume's difficulty; the incompatibility lies between the two principles which he states on the one hand and on the other the unity and continuity of the self, which he feels to be an undeniable datum. In other words, Hume could not reconcile his theory—which left him with a self that had been broken up into perceptions—with the inner feeling of unity and continuity of his own person. This interpretation is based not only on the general context of the appendix but also upon Hume's own declaration that his "account is very defective" when he "proceeds to explain the principle of connexion, which binds

9. *Treatise*, 1, 559.
1. *Ibid*. Hume's italics.

[the perceptions] together." [2] The contradiction becomes clear if we insert the principle of the unity of the self—which Hume had in the back of his mind—between the two principles which he stated in the passage quoted above.

Hume was aware, then, that he had reduced the self to a heap of completely separate fragments and that it was necessary to find a principle by which perceptions might be given unity. He does not propose one, however, although he does consider two possibilities which, in his opinion, would give unity to the self; it seems that he does not accept them because they would imply the very opposite of the two principles which he had already stated. He writes: "Did our perceptions either inhere in something simple and individual, or did the mind perceive some real connexion among them, there would be no difficulty in the case." [3] The first alternative shows that the substantialist principle was still in his mind as a basic possibility for a source of unity, even if he did have to reject it because it had no place within the scheme of his atomist empiricism. The rejection of the second alternative proves that he had a negative attitude with regard to the existence of a continuous self. In the face of this situation Hume takes refuge in the convenient retreat of skepticism; he writes, "For my part, I must plead the privilege of a sceptic, and confess, that this difficulty is too hard for my understanding." [4] He recognizes,

2. *Ibid.*
3. *Ibid.*
4. *Ibid.*

however, that the difficulty is not absolutely insuperable and that other philosophers, or perhaps he himself, after maturer reflection, may possibly be able to solve it.

It is evident that when he wrote the appendix Hume felt the need to seek a unity of perceptions despite the fact that he continued to admit that he could not "perceive any thing but the perceptions." [5] He says that he finds himself "involved in such a labyrinth, that, I must confess, I neither know how to correct my former opinions, nor how to render them consistent." [6]

Why did Hume feel the need to give unity to perceptions? Why did he not leave them as they were at the end of his analysis, in a loose heap? As has been demonstrated, it was not a problem of logical coherence: there is not the slightest incompatibility between the two principles enunciated by Hume. Perhaps a feeling of incompatibility arose in his mind when he compared the results of his analysis with the reality revealed to him by his inner feeling. If a second edition of the *Treatise* had been published within the life of Hume, he would possibly have felt the need to clarify the problem which he set forth in the appendix.[7] As the matter stands, any reply suggested as an answer to the questions formulated above would be nothing more than a conjecture. What does

5. *Ibid.*, 1, 558.
6. *Ibid.*
7. The *Treatise* was not reprinted in English until 1817. It was published in German (*Über die menschliche Natur*, Halle, 1790) by Heinrich Jacob, who was perhaps the first to point out, contrary to Hume's own opinion, that the *Treatise* is superior to the *Enquiry*.

seem to be a fact is that after writing Book I of the *Treatise* he saw things that he had not noticed before; this would account for those passages in the appendix which we have been considering. That the views expressed in those passages are not mere transitory ones might be suspected from the fact that he omits the problem of personal identity from his *Enquiry Concerning Human Understanding,* a work published ten years later (1748) and considered by him to contain his true sentiments and philosophic principles.[8] This suspicion is confirmed by a letter dated 1746 in which he states that his views on personal identity continue to be unsatisfactory to him and expresses his approval of the constructive efforts of Henry Home toward an explanation of personal identity in his *Essays on the Principles of Morality.*[9]

Thus the problem has remained since the time of Hume. All the later empirical solutions have followed either the attitude of the *Treatise* or that of the ap-

8. In the posthumous edition of his *Collected Essays,* published in 1777, there is a note of Hume's in which he refers to the *Treatise* as a "juvenile work" and objects to those who base their attacks against his philosophy upon this work. He adds that the *Enquiry* "may alone be regarded as containing his philosophical sentiments and principles." As we know, Hume was planning the *Treatise* before he left college and wrote it shortly afterward, when he was between twenty-one and twenty-five years old. He finished the work in 1736; the first two books appeared in 1739 and the third in 1740. The *Enquiry Concerning Human Understanding* was published in 1748.

9. Cf. letter to H. Home already cited, in the *Letters of David Hume,* 1, 94.

pendix. Those who adopted the former attitude fell in the same error as Hume did: that one had to choose between the substantialist self and no self at all. Hence the disunity of the self up to the present time. The others attempted the reconstruction recommended by Hume in the appendix and sought the unity of perceptions in the very interstices that separate them. They have proposed hypotheses like so much patchwork because they were capable of perceiving only one-to-one relations. William James is the greatest exponent of these thinkers who saw the insufficiency of Hume's atomism but committed the error of trying to overcome it without abandoning the atomistic attitude.[1]

1. Cf. W. James, "A World of Pure Experience" (1904), reprinted in *Essays in Radical Empiricism* (New York, Longmans, Green, 1912); see especially pp. 41–2 concerning his relation to Hume, and pp. 44–52, concerning the concept of "conjunctive relation" with which he proposes to fill in the gaps left by Hume's atomism.

Part II
EXISTENCE
AND NATURE OF
THE SELF

CHAPTER V

The Problem of the Existence of the Self

1. Meaning of the problem

Even though it has, I think, been shown that the criticism of Hume and his followers does not really refer to the self but is directed against a particular theory of the self, the problem of its existence is still a real one. Proof of the actual existence of the self cannot be deduced from the fallacy of the arguments that would deny it. For a proof to be valid it must be of a positive nature and not based on someone else's mistakes.

Does the self actually exist? Such a general question concerning the existence of the self is too vague to have precise meaning. Any reply that might be given would refer to a definite concept. One affirms or denies this or that *theory* of the self. Hume's case, the classic negation of personal identity which in fact denies the existence of the substantial self, is a good illustration. For the question to make sense, a definite meaning must be affixed to the term "self"; but the reply would then affirm or deny the self only in that particular sense. To make a long enumeration of the different ways of understanding the self, as Bradley does,[1] in order then to affirm the self in one of these meanings or to deny them all is hardly profitable, since in the negative case there is always the possibility that the self may exist in a sense which we had not considered in our list.

What approach is there left? Should we declare that the problem of the self is a pseudo problem, as someone might hastily suggest? Of course not. Reality is extremely complex and involved, and we should not despair just because we can make no progress along the lines that we had originally planned. There is always a new possibility, if one persists in the effort and confronts reality not in order to prove something but rather in order to discover its secrets.

The most adequate approach that I can see and one that reduces the theoretical assumptions to the barest minimum is to ask simply what it is that exists without assuming anything concerning the nature of this "what."

If we direct our gaze inward, the first thing that we notice is our immediate interrogative experience. If we continue to observe this experience, we discover that it does not remain stable, that the interrogation tends sometimes in one direction, sometimes in another; that at times the interrogation seems to ripen into a reply only to abandon that reply and acquire a different significance, a new shade of meaning. This ebb and flow of an intellectual nature is accompanied by emotive and volitive experiences. The interrogation is colored by a feeling of satisfaction when an answer seems to be in the offing and

1. Cf. F. H. Bradley, *Appearance and Reality* (1893), chap. ix.

then is plunged into the depths of weariness or despair. The suffering and despair do not last long; the will urges us to make a new effort, and an intellectual experience comes to the fore in search of a new route.

Both the intellectual experiences and the volitive or emotive ones are, as we shall see, very closely interrelated, not only among themselves but also with the other types of experience. At the same time, they maintain an intimate relationship with all the past experiences, but this matter, too, we shall lay aside for the time being. What concerns the concrete problem which we are now considering is the empirical proof—by simple introspective observation—of the existence of experiences that alter their nature or are displaced by other experiences that we may have.

If anyone doubts that experiences exist, his very doubt will provide us with the reason: doubt presupposes a dubitative experience which, by its presence, illustrates the fact that experiences exist. Descartes has demonstrated once and for all the impossibility of doubting the existence of our cogitationes.[2]

We have now established one fact: the existence of experiences is indubitable. The problem can now be stated meaningfully and in rigorous terms. Can our psychic life be reduced to the sum of our experiences, or is there something more, an unknown x (whatever its na-

2. For the present we shall use as synonyms the terms "cogitatio" as employed by Descartes, "perception" by Hume, or "experience" (Erlebnis) by contemporary German philosophy to express a psychological state, whatever its nature.

ture may be), that is not an experience or the equivalent of the sum of our experiences?

The problem can be resolved neither dogmatically nor deductively. One must take two fundamental precautions in examining reality: on the one hand, to be quite careful that no fact of an unknown variety—just what we are searching for—escapes our notice or hides within the tangled mass of experiences; on the other, to sharpen our critical capacity so that, in our great eagerness to find what we are hunting for, we do not hypostatize something that does not exist and then attempt to "discover" what we have already presupposed.

2. Is the self an intuitive datum?

Some readers will perhaps object that this search for the self is a waste of time because "everyone knows by intuition" that his self exists and such knowledge is immediate and unquestionable. Others may arrive at a similar conclusion by thinking it "self-evident" that experiences must be the experiences of *someone*. Both these attitudes may be observed not only in hasty or impatient readers but also in philosophers who have spent a great deal of time studying the problem. I shall not analyze the attitude of the second group because it is an echo of the substantialist prejudice that I have criticized repeatedly and because the argument is valueless since it begs the question: it presupposes exactly what must be demonstrated.

The first argument, however, is new to us. It is a popular version of a doctrine we cannot disregard and that maintains the existence of a cognitive instrument—the intuition [3]—which in an immediate and absolute way makes us aware of the presence of the self. In contemporary philosophy Bergson is its most ardent supporter. This very subtle and acute philosopher, in analyzing the inner life, passes over the problem with the assurance of one who considers it a waste of time to demonstrate what is a primary and self-evident datum. He begins his *Creative Evolution* with the statement that there is nothing of which we are so sure as of our own existence, "for of every other object we have notions which may be considered external and superficial, whereas, of ourselves, our perception is internal and profound." [4] When, in the second paragraph, he goes on to analyze his existence, he enumerates the various types of experiences [5] and then affirms, with no further examination, the existence of a self which changes but does not cease; [6] for a self that does not change does not endure. [7] This deliberate ignoring of the problem, which we see in *Creative Evolution*, is supported by an expressly stated attitude found

3. Despite the differences of opinion that exist among the various philosophers concerning what the word "intuition" should mean, all of those who use this concept seem to agree that it connotes direct and immediate apprehension. It is in this sense that I use the word, except when referring directly to a particular philosopher.

4. Bergson, *Creative Evolution*, tr. A. Mitchell (New York, 1911), p. 1.

5. "Sensations, feelings, volitions, ideas—such are the changes into which my existence is divided." *Ibid.*

6. *Ibid.*

7. *Ibid.*, p. 4.

in the *Introduction to Metaphysics* where he writes: "There is one reality, at least, which we all seize from within, by intuition and not by simple analysis. It is our own personality in its flowing through time—our self which endures [*dure*]." [8] Such an intuitive apprehension of the self seems to provide an absolute knowledge: "an inner, absolute knowledge of the duration of the self by the self is possible." [9]

What is this reality that Bergson calls "our own personality" which we grasp by intuition? It seems evident that the self cannot constitute the totality of the object grasped by the intuition, for it is always accompanied by its experiences. When we intuit its presence we intuit at the same time the concrete experiences that accompany it. How can we be sure that we are not actually intuiting the experiences, and influenced by the persistently attractive presupposition that qualities cannot exist per se, are we not hypostatizing the existence of the self?

Besides, intuition cannot reveal to us the presence of the self without telling us something concerning its nature, however obscure and confused the data and circumstances may be. In other words, the data on the existence of what we intuit are intimately connected with certain data on its nature so that we can correct certain details but not the essential aspects. Such is the case in external perception. We can make a mistake concerning a per-

8. Bergson, *An Introduction to Metaphysics*, tr. T. E. Hulme (New York, 1912), p. 9.

9. *Ibid.*, p. 24.

son that we perceive in the distance, but, in spite of the mistake, the fact still remains that we perceive a person or a living being or an object that moves. The perception of the existence of a "thing" cannot be *completely* separated from the perception of its nature, no matter how vague the latter may be.

One cannot, consequently, be sure about the existence of the self without making reference, at least to some extent, to its constitutive nature. Since this is so, all those who intuit the self should agree on some basic common element, though there remains the possibility that they may disagree in other respects. As a matter of fact, however, if one compares the descriptions given by the various philosophers who claim to intuit the existence of the self, one will discover, in many cases, complete disagreement. There are those who think that they intuit it as a simple immutable substance, others, on the contrary, as an essentially changing reality. If the intuitive data concerning the constitutive nature of the self are not definite—for one or the other of the two above-stated contradictory intuitions must be false—one may suspect that the supposed datum concerning its presence may also be erroneous, since existence cannot be entirely divorced from constitutive nature.

The difference of opinion in the so-called intuitive field extends further still. There have been philosophers, from Hume to James, who have stated that they possess a direct awareness of the *non*existence of the self. In his examination of the inner life, Hume discovers only "perceptions," and William James, whose capacity for psychological self-analysis cannot be denied, writes at the end of his famous article, "Does Consciousness Exist?":

> I, too, have my intuitions and I must obey them. Let the case be what it may in others, I am as confident as I am of anything that, in myself, the stream of thinking (which I recognize emphatically as a phenomenon) is only a careless name for what, when scrutinized, reveals itself to consist chiefly of the stream of my breathing. The "I think" which Kant said must be able to accompany all my objects, is the "I breathe" which actually does accompany them.[1]

Although I do not agree with James, who in the passage quoted proves only that the philosophic doctrine which one professes interferes with the supposed immediate apprehension of our inner life, I cannot take the opposite position and dogmatically state that as far as I am concerned there exists a true intuition of the presence of the self. In so doing, I should run the risk of making the same mistake by giving the name of "immediate datum of consciousness" to what at bottom is a mere *idolum theatri.*

In other words, the question cannot be legitimately resolved by affirming or denying the existence in ourselves of this intuitive capacity that reveals to us in an immediate fashion the presence of the self. In the first place, what concerns us is not the existence of our individual self—although we refer to it constantly as the most valuable

1. James, *Essays in Radical Empiricism*, pp. 36–7.

and accessible source at our disposal—but the self of every human being. And the testimony of a man like James is worth just as much as that of another man, like Bergson. Secondly, neither of them stands alone; with slight variations and shades of meaning they are supported by many other philosophers. Moreover, if I restrict my observation to my own individual self, I discover, as a matter of fact, an intuition that reveals its presence; but my own experience has taught me to be wary of such intuitions, for more than once, in similar circumstances, I have afterward discovered the concealed door through which the content of my supposed intuition had entered into my consciousness. We find, moreover, that the most ardent defenders of intuition as a form of absolute cognition frequently write that they have had varying intuitions during their lives and that a later intuition nullifies the certainty and accuracy of the former ones. What criterion can be adopted in order to decide whether the last intuition is in fact the true one? It may be the first intuition or any of those in between or—as is most probable—none of them at all.

A thoroughgoing examination shows us, moreover, that in many cases the intuitive data conform too closely to the previously held conceptual pattern. In a word, the immediacy of intuitive apprehension is highly dubious; intuition apparently does not overcome the classic difficulties of introspection. The existence of individuals who suffer from dual personality or who really believe that they are the reincarnations of historic personages augments our distrust and demonstrates again the necessity for adopting a cautious attitude with regard to the supposed intuitive evidence of the self.

This does not mean, of course, that we should ignore intuitive data. From the fallibility of intuition its critics have deduced that such data lack all validity; in so doing they commit an inexcusable error in logic and deprive themselves of a valuable instrument for the cognition of the inner life. Both the advocates of intuition and their opponents commit the same kind of error. The former base their conclusion on the positive instances only, ignoring all the cases in which intuition has failed; the latter, on the other hand, take into account only the negative cases, as if one who tells a lie can never speak the truth.

What one should do is to recognize that intuition—and its sophisticated theoretical forms such as the "immanent perception" of Husserl—does not yield us absolute knowledge of infallible data but is a source of knowledge like sense perception, the fallibility of which, though recognized by everyone, has not impaired its importance. The lack of absolute forms of knowledge forces us to attack reality by all the means at our disposal, no matter how imperfect they are, if we actually want to unravel any of its secrets. In the particular case of intuition we must compare the data of different intuitions with one another and then compare these intuitions with the other forms of experience and with the theories consciously held. In the case of James, for example, one might apply to him his own pragmatic method and show that his behavior, which contains an implicit doctrine, does not agree with what he calls his intuition. James' case is not one of intuition, if we mean by intuition a direct and immediate apprehension of something given, but the result of a long process of reasoning concealed by an ingenious and biting literary presentation.

3. Evidences of the existence of the self

If intuition does not provide us with decisive data to support the existence of the self, some other way should be tried to confirm or deny the intuitive data. The most adequate method I can think of is to examine concrete psychological situations and find out whether or not we can explain them wholly in terms of experiences, which are the only reality we have found so far. If not we should admit the existence of something more than the "heap of perceptions."

Suppose I am reading a book—Whitehead's *Process and Reality*, for instance. I read the first part where Whitehead gives the basic ideas. Now I am reading the second part which is to be understood in relation to the first. Could I understand it if all the experiences I had when I read the first part were gone? My past experiences are present in some way; otherwise every time I read a passage of a book the experience would be new and the process of learning impossible. But we *do* learn; we *do* understand a subsequent chapter which is based on the first. Could these facts be explained in a world of disconnected experiences such as the one described by Hume? [2] Cer-

2. We must remember that for Hume, and for many of his contemporary followers, the self is "nothing but a bundle or col-

tainly not. In such a world a past experience is gone forever; it has been replaced by the present one. Moreover, according to Hume, our experiences (perceptions) are different from each other and may exist separately, having no need of anything else to support their existence.[3] In fact, we need some kind of permanence and continuity to make the process of understanding or learning possible.

Bertrand Russell and some of his followers do not seem to accept the validity of this argument. "Perhaps it is the nerves that acquire experience rather than the mind. If so, the possibility of acquiring experience cannot be used to define mind." [4]

Should Russell be right, cases of understanding, learn-

---

lection of different perceptions, which succeed each other with an inconceivable rapidity, and are in a perpetual flux and movement. Our eyes cannot turn in their sockets without varying our perceptions. Our thought is still more variable than our sight; and all our other senses and faculties contribute to this change; nor is there any single power of the soul, which remains unalterably the same, perhaps for one moment. The mind is a kind of theatre, where several perceptions successively make their appearance; pass, re-pass, glide away, and mingle in an infinite variety of postures and situations. There is properly no *simplicity* in it at one time, nor *identity* in different; whatever natural propension we may have to imagine that simplicity and identity. The comparison of the theatre must not mislead us. They are the successive perceptions only, that constitute the mind . . ." Cf. *Treatise*, I, iv, 6 (1, 534).

3. Cf. *ibid.*, I, iv, 5 (1, 518).

4. B. Russell, *The Analysis of Mind* (London, George Allen and Unwin, 1933), p. 295.

ing, and memory will be no evidence of the existence of something besides experiences. Memory and learning are possible, according to him, because of the existence of the nervous tissue which is altered at each experience.[5] This physiological explanation of psychological events will finally lead us to a physical explanation. Does not magnetized iron show a different "behavior" from ordinary iron? If one can speak of "the experiences of the nervous tissue," one can very well discuss the "experiences of magnetized iron."

In order to keep the discussion concentrated on the main point of this chapter, let us admit that learning, understanding, and memory are not evidences of the existence of something besides the mere experiences, and let us turn to some other psychological facts that neither Hume's nor Russell's doctrines seem to explain. Let us examine, for example, a case of decision.

All of a sudden we decide to shift from the profession we have followed for years to a different one. Our previous experiences and behavior could not make anyone anticipate such a decision. The profession we had easily covered our family needs. In addition to our advantageous economic situation, we enjoyed a good social and professional reputation, and everyone was pleased with what we were doing. Notwithstanding, we decided to throw away years of study and hard practice, an economic, social, and professional position honestly reached, and take the risk of a new and hazardous profession. How is this decision possible? If we were nothing but a stream of experiences or

5. Cf. *Ibid.*, pp. 293–5, and chap. iv.

a nervous system, the future should be determined by the past. But in the case we are discussing, our decision was not determined by our past experiences. In fact, it opposed them. It is true that our decision was not completely disconnected from our previous experiences, but it is also true that the decision was not the blind result of the pressure of past experiences. And such a case is not unique. In fact, it is what happens every time an important decision is made. One who is adrift in a world of disconnected experiences, or is pushed one way or the other by them, does not know what a real decision means. Such decisions are mere consequences of what has previously happened. But the case we are discussing is different. Previous experiences were pushing us the old way. Then, all of a sudden, we decided to impose a new direction to our lives. We did not follow the experiential stream; we anticipated its course, so to speak. Could we say, in such a case, that it is the experiential stream or the nervous system which has decided? In a world without "something more" than a mere aggregate of experiences, decision is meaningless; everything is inexorably determined by the past.

If cases of decisions show the presence of something which cannot be reduced to past experiences, what about religious conversions? How can we explain them unless we admit the existence of something permanent that gives sense and unity to such experiences?

Let us examine a third situation: a case of repentance. Misunderstanding the meaning of a friend's behavior, we hurt his feelings. When later we think it over, we find we were not fair to him and we repent of what we did. The situation could, of course, be more complicated, but the case just described suffices. Could repentance be possible if we were a "heap of different perceptions," as Hume describes us? Who could repent if every past experience were gone forever?

Numerous other instances can be offered as evidences of the existence of "something more" than the experiences, a *plus* which can be reduced neither to an experience nor to the experiential stream and which we usually call the "self." Besides learning, decision, and repentance many other psychological facts could be included, namely promise, self-respect, hope, humiliation, dignity, worry. How could we, for example, be worried about our own future, the future of our country or of our children, if we were only a heap of passing experiences? It is true that to be worried means to have an experience just as in cases of decision and repentance. But such an experience could not exist unless behind the coming and going of the experiences something permanent exists which explains the possibility of anticipating future experiences. The same is true of promise, and that is why man was once defined as "the animal that can make a promise."

The concrete psychological situations to which we have been referring could not exist if the self was nothing but a discontinued reality constituted by the mechanical adjustment of experiences. That is why it is necessary to admit the existence of something which is intimately connected to the experiences but which is not equivalent to the mere sum of them and which gives stability, unity, meaning, and continuity to the experiential stream. We

may call the self, then, this *plus* which is not hidden behind the experiences but which cannot be identified with
any one of them.

The self not only exists but we are even conscious of
its existence; it is the so-called self-consciousness which is
one of the main characteristics of human life. The self
sees and knows that it sees; it is happy and knows that it is
happy; it hopes and knows that it hopes. It is conscious
not only of particular experiences but also of the unity and
continuity of itself. We know that the one who is reading this page is the same person that has read the previous
page and the same that has taken this book into his hands.
These immediate data of the consciousness of the continuity of ourselves through change are also given to the
minds of men such as Hume, who realizes that his theory
does not explain "the principles that unite our successive
perceptions in our thought or consciousness." Our discussion of the two principles which Hume could not
reconcile seems to prove it.[6]

If anybody holds that he is not conscious of the continuity of himself since he perceives himself as a changing
being, we could show him that such a statement implies
a contradiction because he could not perceive his changing self unless there is something permanent in him that
perceives the changes and something that constantly remains which he can use as a point of reference. We realize
we change because there is something in us that is constant. Should a person change completely he would not
realize that he has changed. As a matter of fact, he would

6. Cf. chap. iv above, pp. 102–6.

not have changed but would have been replaced by a different person who would have nothing in common with the previous one. The lack of connection between the two would make them two different persons instead of a changing one.

The presence of the self is evident particularly in cases of strain, opposition, and struggle. In an easy life without trouble, in moments of peace and tranquillity, the self hides itself behind the smooth and gentle experiential stream. But a sudden interruption of the common flow of life is enough to show the presence of the self that emerges from the experiential stream and does not let it flow but leads it. It is at such time that the self stops drifting with the current of the experiential flux and imposes its will, determines a goal, and indicates the way of reaching that goal.

Memory and will, past and future, need the presence of the self to give them meaning. In hundreds of cases it will be easy to show that many psychological situations would be incomprehensible if we deny the self. It will suffice to add that moral behavior and moral problems would be meaningless if we drop the self. How would responsibility be possible, for instance? Who would be responsible for a crime? The experience at the moment it was done? The whole of the experiential flux? Or simply the Ego that committed the crime?

Opposition to the existence of the self is due, as we pointed out in the case of Hume, to a misleading way of stating the problem. Both substantialists and antisubstantialists think the only chance there is of having a self is the substantial self, the res cogitans. Some fight for it, some against it, but both are blinded by its supposed presence. There are still many thinkers who do not want to admit anything that may be called a self or an Ego, simply because they find that the self changes, that there is no immutable core within it. And, as they have observed that change is an essential characteristic of our experience, they arrive at the conclusion that the self is nothing but a collection of experiences. They fail to recognize the fact that "change" is of quite a different character when it is referred to the experiences than when it is referred to the self. Experiences change by substitution; in the experiential flux one experience takes the place of the other. The experience of sorrow that I now have because I received bad news has taken the place of the experience of joy that I had a moment ago. Sorrow is not a modification of joy; it is simply a new experience. The same can be said of different experiences of one particular kind. Each shade in an experience means a *new* experience. Something quite different happens to the self. It changes not by substitution but by alteration; whenever it changes it undergoes an inner adjustment. That is why it can change and be the same, as we shall see in the next two chapters.

CHAPTER VI

Self and Function

1. *The substantialist doctrine of the self*

It has been shown in the preceding chapter that the self is not an *ignis fatuus* but a reality, an undeniable fact and not a metaphysical hypostasis. It has been proved, I think, that one cannot discover an experience that is neither mine nor yours, that does not belong to an Ego. The self is associated with the stream of experiences from beginning to end and is never found to be absent; its presence is constant, its permanence necessary. Now the problem is to analyze its nature.

The atomists, in their eagerness to criticize substance as a metaphysical postulate, confused an interpretive doctrine of the self with the very self and discarded them both, leaving our inner life entirely disintegrated. This seemed to contradict not only the intimate conviction of those who were opposed to atomism but also that of the very ones who supported it. So everyone feverishly began the work of reconstructing what had been torn to pieces by too hasty and extreme an analysis. The atomists tried to reconstitute the unity and continuity of the self by a process of summation in which only the relationship of member to member is taken into account. Thus they finally conceived of the self as a chain of experiences. All the links are united because each one of them is joined to the one that precedes it and to the one that follows. The result was a mechanized self that seemed more like a robot than a man, for it lacked spontaneous reactions, creative direction, life. At best, they conceived of the self as a passive movie screen upon which is projected an uninterrupted stream of images which have little or no effect upon the screen.

Since it could not reconstitute the unity and continuity that it had destroyed, atomistic empiricism was not found satisfactory, and attempts were made to find a basis for unity outside of experience. Thus there arose the concepts of "consciousness in general" (*Bewusstsein überhaupt*) and "pure self," and the postulate of spiritual substance in turn regained its lost prestige. If the data of empirical life reveal to us a self that is disconnected, it was thought necessary to look to the superempirical realm for something that would connect the different members and satisfy our intimate intuitions, which tell us that the self is a unity and not an amorphous mass of disconnected experiences, a continuous fact and not an intermittent series of transitory states. It was not realized that atomism is a naïve and primitive form of empiricism—as is sensationalism—and that one can be empirical without being atomistic. What is more, a true empiricism necessitates the repudiation of the abstractions of atomism. In other words, there is no need to step outside of the empirical world to find the unity of the self that atomism had destroyed. It is, then, a deficient empiricism that is responsible for so many relapses into ingenious but fruitless metaphysical doctrines concerning the self.

Of all the superempirical beings postulated to give unity to the self, the most satisfactory was substance. It solved the difficulties that atomism had caused. The unity and continuity of the self were explained by the unity and continuity of substance, its changes by the modifications that the attributes, modes, and qualities could undergo.

Substantialism, moreover, allowed one to conceive of the self after the fashion of a physical reality and thus brought it closer to the attitude of common sense, which maintains that "seeing is believing." At the same time, it coincided with the popular doctrine of the soul, according to which, although a spiritual nature is attributed to it verbally, the soul is interpreted in terms that betray a static, physical, passive concept.

It is true that it is not easy to find contemporary philosophers who are in complete agreement with the classic substantialist conception of the self as an immutable, simple, and independent being. There are, nevertheless, many thinkers who support one or another of these characteristics. Most common is immutability. Perhaps fearing lest the empirical examination of the self dissolve into nothingness that which they most desire to preserve, they postulate the existence of a substantial, immutable nucleus that is completely unaffected by the modifications that might be brought about by the most violent changes in our inner life.

Let us choose for analysis a case that seems to be typical—that of an acute thinker who is familiar with the empirical doctrine extending from Hume to James and who, after making all sorts of concessions to this doctrine, seizes upon a substantial nucleus like a man who, in the last throes of drowning, suddenly discovers a life preserver nearby. I refer to DeWitt H. Parker; I shall examine his doctrine as it is presented in his work, *Experience and Substance*.[1]

Parker states that he is adopting from the very beginning an empirical method and promises to discard all theory of the self as something that exists outside of experience.[2] In his first approach to the subject he adopts an attitude similar to that of Hume, James, and Mach, as he himself admits.[3] In the following lines, however, we see his objection:

> But to all such views there is this important objection, that they seem to reduce the self, which is intuitively a unity, to a bare multiplicity of factors. For,

1. This is not the first time that Parker has been concerned with the problem of the self. He devoted to the same problem a good portion of an earlier book of his entitled *The Self and Nature* (Cambridge, Harvard University Press, 1917). We prefer to examine his doctrine rather than those that admit a substantialist self for religious reasons, for it shows on a purely theoretical level the influence of false dilemmas upon philosophers' ideas and the dangers of an incomplete empiricism, which serves only to throw those who practice it back to a metaempirical realm.

2. Parker, *Experience and Substance* (Ann Arbor, University of Michigan Press, 1941), p. 28.

3. *Ibid.*, p. 41.

whether these factors be denominated thoughts, activities, elements, or impressions, they are many, and if we view the self as made up out of them it appears to be, as Plato said of it, a society rather than a unity, in fact almost a crowd.[4]

Such an objection leads to what Parker calls "a crisis in the analysis of the self."[5] On one hand we have the multiplicity of experiences, on the other the unity and "endurance" of the self. Parker decides upon the second alternative and, although the process is a slow one, we can anticipate the result as soon as we know the route he has chosen.

Parker distinguishes between what he calls "focal self" and "matrix self." The former consists of the activity or the aggregate of activities going on at a given moment —present thought, impulse, etc. The focal self is an event, a coming and going, one in the series of events that appear and disappear. These events, however, do not arise from nothingness; they are oriented with reference to something deeper and more stable than they. Every intelligible relationship that they have with one another is derived from the matrix from which they have arisen.

The matrix self supplies the stability that the self possesses and which cannot be found in the focal self. Is this matrix self changing or immutable for Parker? His answer is: "I do not wish to imply that the matrix self is changeless; but the fact is that it moves more slowly

4. *Ibid.*
5. *Ibid.*, p. 42.

than the pulse of focal activities." [6] And he adds that each focal activity alters the matrix self by enriching it and causing in it an inner adjustment. So far we have no objections to make, for his description agrees with experience. What we do not see is how he is going to manage to explain in this way unity and permanence, which is what he had set out to do. The author, too, seems to notice this difficulty, for he suddenly changes tactics and chooses a course which in its own way will assure him of unity and permanence but will cut him off completely from experience. He writes: "The matrix self never changes entirely—there is a core which remains the same over long periods of time, indeed as long as the self endures." [7] This core or unchanging nucleus of the matrix self Parker calls the "essential self." [8]

What is this central core but the postulation of a metaphysical being in order to stave off an infinite regress? His focal self is changeable and finds its stability in the matrix self; but as the matrix self must also change since the activities of the focal self modify it, it becomes necessary to introduce another hypothetical self—as supports of the matrix self—for the stability being sought after. What is the "essential self" but an immutable *je ne sais quoi* which merely serves to give stability to the matrix self? Is not this doctrine the same as the Hindu's theory of which Locke tells us—an elephant holding up

6. *Ibid.*, pp. 44–5.
7. *Ibid.*, p. 45.
8. The proofs that he promises on p. 45 and gives us on pp. 60–7 do nothing further to illuminate the problem.

the earth, a tortoise holding up the elephant, and a *je ne sais quoi* holding up the tortoise? This is a spurious argument resorted to for the purpose of staving off an infinite regress that should never have been started in the first place. If the *je ne sais quoi* needs nothing to hold it up, why should the earth need something? And if the latter needs a support, the former needs one too, as is the case with the matrix and the essential selves.

By the same token, why should one have to go looking into an area far away from experience in order to find an explanation for unity and permanence of the self? Why cannot the activities support themselves, forming a self-contained framework that needs no mysterious essential self? How do we apprehend the essential self? In what relationships does it stand with regard to the matrix and focal selves? Despite the fact that Parker states that such relationships do exist because the three are but aspects of a single self,[9] it is not here made evident what sort of relationships they have. Focal activities alter the matrix self; what happens to the matrix self must affect in turn the essential self. Otherwise, the relationship between the three could not be intimate, as is stated; the essential self would be the core of a surrounding matter that is completely foreign to it. Thus, everything that happens to us, all our efforts toward education and self-improvement, repentance and conversion, would be meaningless, for that central core would remain untouched by all the storms that may take place in our life.

Whence comes the essence of this essential self? If

9. *Ibid.*, p. 45.

what happens to us does not change it, it is evidently not an "essence" formed by sedimentation from the experiences that we have undergone. There remains only the possibility of innate existence, a gift of Providence at the moment of conception. Such a hypothesis would have to be rejected at once, not only for lack of empirical support but also because of its ethical consequences. It would imply the acceptance of a blind fate, which would make responsibility, education, and self-improvement mere illusions.

We understand, nevertheless, the reason that Parker and many other like-minded philosophers have for postulating an irreducible and immutable core. It arises from a desire to solve the crisis of which Parker speaks, to end, once and for all, the process of dissolution which seems to threaten to reduce the self to a mere sum of its successive states. In other words, they feel the need to *save*, at any cost, the unity and permanence of the self, which are threatened by a halfway empirical attitude.

Setting aside Parker's doctrine, we may still ask, in a general way, what other reasons can be brought forward in favor of the thesis of the immutability of the self. What means of access do we have to this irreducible core? How can we recognize the existence of such a core and its immutability? It seems evident that empirical examination reveals the mutability of the self. Not much psychological insight is necessary for one to realize that he is different than he was as a child, that he likes things now that he did not like formerly and is bored by what delighted him most in his childhood; he knows things now that he did not know before, he desires what he formerly did not desire, he is able to do what he formerly could not do. The final end and purpose of our life is different from that of our childhood.

I am not trying to maintain that the self is essentially mutable but rather to point out one characteristic of the self revealed to us by empirical examination which denies the supposed immutability of the self. But this is only one aspect of the self, for the immediate data of our consciousness reveal to us in the same way a single and continuous self, assuring us that in spite of changes we are the same person that we were in our childhood. This consciousness of the permanent nature of our self that enters into all our actions is just as empirical a datum as the one that tells us of the coming and going of experiences. Nevertheless, though still an immediate datum, it is a more complex one and is more difficult to reconcile with the interpretation of atomistic empiricism.

We are different without ceasing to be the same. The whole difficulty seems to rest on the explanation of endurance through change. Empiricism concentrates upon change and is unable to explain permanence. Substantialism is more concerned with permanence and relegates change to a superficial level by postulating an immutable self surrounded by a superficial, changing shell. Both are thinking of a static, rigid personal identity that defies alteration—empiricism in order to attack it, substantialism in order to relegate to a secondary plane whatever seems to deny it. The need to explain personal identity and thus save man from psychological and moral chaos seems to be the fundamental reason for the substantialist postulate.

Is such a postulate justifiable? The self is an empirical reality, and our explanations of it must have an empirical basis. Within a sane philosophical system one has no right to postulate metaphysical beings which serve to fill in the gaps left by an inadequate empirical analysis. Solutions must be sought within experience itself; we should not give free rein to our speculative imagination lest we devise a very coherent system that solves all the problems on a theoretical level but has absolutely nothing to do with the reality that we are trying to understand, describe, and explain.

In this chapter I want to concentrate upon criticizing the doctrine of the immutability of the self in order to make more evident its functional nature. It is my belief that everything that happens to us has a repercussion, to a greater or less degree, upon the totality of our being. There is no nucleus or substratum that is totally separated from the other layers that constitute the self. This criticism of immutability will occasionally bring us close to atomistic empiricism, which in turn I shall criticize in the following chapter where I shall also set forth a doctrine to explain the unity, permanence, and continuity of the self without denying its changing nature.

If the self were really constituted of a substantial, immutable nucleus that underlay what happens to us and what we observe in the world of experience, how would we characterize a person, a particular self? By the hidden nucleus that we cannot know, or by what that person has done, does, and is able to do? It seems to me that it will have to be by the second means, for the first lies outside of experience, and we only know that it is "something" that "supports" experiences. At least, so it is in everyday life, in which judges and confessors condemn or absolve the accused, before the tribunal of the law or of conscience, on the basis of what has been done and of past and future intentions. The supposed irreducible nucleus is never brought into the case, except perhaps for metaphorical purposes. And it could not be otherwise, for if his actions and intentions deserve condemnation, the accused could not possibly be acquitted on the basis that he has an irreducible core of hypothetical goodness. Among other reasons, we do not understand how the judge or confessor could possibly find out about the existence of such a core and what its specific nature was.

And we cannot, of course, ignore the moral consequences that would result from the postulation of an immutable nucleus that constituted the essence of our self. Why should we be educated? Why should we make an effort to improve ourselves? Why should we teach and preach what we consider good? A life of vice, selfishness, or even crime would have the same value as a life spent in pursuit of the good, a life full of self-sacrifice, unselfishness, neighborly love. Both would leave the self unchanged, just as it was to begin with. Thus all possibility of real education, of culpability, repentance, and responsibility would vanish automatically. If our nucleus is immutable we must suppose that it is born with us and that we are not, therefore, responsible for it because of its origin and the impossibility of changing it.

In order to avoid this type of criticism—which would finally result in the *reductio ad absurdum* of the substantialist conception—the advocates of the doctrine of substance have made an effort to maintain an equilibrium between substance itself and its essential attribute. The history of philosophy presents us with a complete scale of delicately shaded distinctions, running all the way from the dominance of substance and relegation of attribute to the status of a casual accident to the dominance of the attribute to such an extent that it reduces the substance to a mere "nothing" that "supports"—who knows by what magic art?—the attribute, which is what really matters. But if the substance is nothing in itself and merely depends upon its essential attribute, it is impossible to see what reality it can have, how we can recognize it, and what purpose its postulation can serve. What is left is a word that with the passage of time has been emptied of all content and is now a mere symbol of past glory. When the word has been reduced to this extent, whether we keep it or not is a matter of literary taste and not of philosophical importance. But it is a prudent measure of philosophic hygiene to throw overboard concepts that have lost their meaning and real content.

If the substantialist conception has so little foundation, how can it have been adhered to for so long a time? In the first place, it has been considered a logical necessity. It has been believed inconceivable that experiences could exist in themselves, for all activity presupposes a subject.

This reason, of an a priori nature, receives confirmation from observations of an empirical sort—though poorly interpretated—and from the failure of antisubstantialist doctrines in their attempt to explain the unity and continuity of the self. Frequently the errors of one doctrine are taken as positive arguments in favor of the opposite thesis. The primary source of support for the substantialist doctrine is the fact that it makes clear the existence of the self. The existence of the self has become so closely associated with the idea of substance that whenever the latter has been attacked it has been thought necessary to deny the former. And, in turn, whenever the self has been duly recognized as existing this recognition has brought in its wake the substantialist interpretation.

2. Permanence and immutability

On the other hand, the observation of the permanent character of the self has been considered proof of its immutable nature. Its permanence, in the sense of constant presence, seems to be an undeniable fact: actually, we can never discover an experience that does not belong to an Ego. The self is always present, but its presence does not indicate a substantial nature or immutability. The very truth that in the presence of a friend we have a self to deal with and not a disjunct aggregate of experiences does not prove anything concerning the immutability of our friend. It is possible that this man may have changed, that he may now have a different religious creed, political conviction, artistic taste, profession, and Weltanschauung, that the bond of friendship formerly uniting us may have been destroyed, that he may express himself in a different language, have a new nationality, etc. Despite all this, we say that we are dealing with the same man. We mean that, though our friend has changed, he has not been replaced by another individual. This seems to prove, according to substantialism, that change is of little importance, for it is the same man despite the change. Again, the unity and continuity of the same individual seem to support the arguments of the substantialists.

The error lies in confusing permanence with immutability. In the case of the self, permanence not only is not incompatible with change but actually presupposes change. A man continues to be the same one, not in spite of the change but because he does undergo changes. If he did not change, he would not be a living human being but would be a dead one. This is a fact that neither atomism nor substantialism could really comprehend: what happens to us modifies the structure of the self but at the same time is that which gives it stability. We are neither pure change nor pure stability but constitute a reality which, in order to be, must become. No one has ever denied the changing nature of the self. The only thing that has been done is to relegate change to a level of secondary or tertiary importance and to allow it merely incidental significance. Who could deny that we change, that the loss of a friend or a son, failure or success, produce an alteration in us, a modification of our being?

What has not been seen is that it is those very facts modifying the self which give it stability. Thus, when we lose a son or a friend, the psychological states that accompany these misfortunes will make us change—we shall no longer be the same man as before—but simultaneously they will so shape our personality that from then on we shall be the man who has lost a child or a friend. Any children that we may have in the future, the new friendships that may enter into our life, will possibly lessen our grief, but they cannot completely erase the spiritual shock produced by such blows. The force of these changes will suffer ebbs and floods, but can never be completely eliminated, for, strictly speaking, they are not external elements that have modified the self but elements that have become constituent members of the very self.

Other facts, too, seem to favor the substantialist view. It is actually observed that the self has a degree of stability that contrasts with the constant flux of experiences. These experiences seem to be states of the self and not its constituent elements, for self and experiences differ in their nature. This argument is deceptive, however, for the constituent elements of a whole do not necessarily possess the same qualities as the whole; as a matter of fact, they rarely possess them. Does an army have a heart, lungs, feet, and hands as do the soldiers that constitute it? Likewise, we do not say that a symphony is not formed by the sounds that make it up just because these sounds are very unstable compared to the relative permanence of the symphony taken as a whole. The soldiers change, but there can be no army without soldiers; the sounds succeed one another in constant change, but there cannot be a symphony if there are no sounds. In the same way our experiences change and follow on the heels of one another, sometimes in headlong flight, but there can be no self without experiences.

We have passed from the examination of a concrete theory to a criticism of substantialism in general. It is obviously impossible to examine all the theories and their variants that come under the heading of substantialism. Besides, more important than the study of explicit doctrines is the critical examination of the whole body of presuppositions that underly them and determine the direction of the philosophic thought of an era. Such is the purpose of the historical examination given in the first part of this book—that the reader may realize the extent of our divergence with the substantialists and the value of the new ideas, which, although they have not yet attained their full degree of maturity, offer a greater fertility than the old doctrines, carefully systematized century after century.

The substantialist position, then, lacks an empirical basis, and there is no reason to consider it a necessary prerequisite for thought. Reduced as it is to a mere support for the qualities or attributes, the postulation of substance not only adds nothing to what we already know from experience but actually takes much away and is, therefore, prejudicial.

3. *The being and the doing of the self*

Experience shows us that the self does not depend upon any obscure or hidden substantial core but depends upon what it does, has done, proposes to do, or is able to do. The self is revealed in its action; it reveals itself and constitutes itself by acting. It is nothing before acting, and nothing remains of it if experiences cease completely. Its *esse* is equivalent to its *facere*. We are not given a ready-made self; we create our own self daily by what we do, what we experience. Our behavior—in which both our actual doing and our intentions should properly be included—is not an expression of our self but the very stuff which constitutes it.

What holds experiences together, what gives us personality, is not, therefore, a substantial bond but a functional one, a coordinated structure of activities. The self is not something already made but something that is always in the making. It is formed throughout the course of its life, just as any institution is formed—a family, a university, a nation. There is no aboriginal nucleus of the self that exists prior to its actions; the self arises and takes on existence as it acts, as it undergoes experiences. The category of substance must be supplanted by that of function if we wish to interpret adequately the nature of the self. The concept of function connotes, in this case, the concepts of activity, process, and relation.

The functional link by no means includes only our past experiences. The self is memory, but it is not memory alone. Our personality depends upon what has happened to us, but it cannot be reduced to our personal history; the self is not the blind aggregate of our experiences. We get the push of the past, but we also get the pull of the future. There is, in the self, a note of novelty and creativity, a free will, an ability to control the eventual course of our experiences. Activity, therefore, contains an element of novelty; it cannot be grasped or comprehended by referring exclusively to its past. The self is not inert matter, deposited on the shore by the tide of experience, but creative will, plotting its own course for itself. It depends upon its past history but is able to mold its own history-to-be, to orient its life according to new courses. It is memory but memory projected toward the future, memory hurled ahead. The future conditions the nature of our self not only as it merges with the present but also while it is still more distantly future. What we plan to do, even if we never get to do it, gives sense to our activities. The future, however, is not a part of our self merely as a system of ideas and intentions; it also enters into the formation of the self through our emotions. In times of confusion and disaster the thought of the future of our country, our child, our own lives grieves us. Though it is true that this suffering is a present and not a future experience, its object is the future. It is like the pain caused by a splinter; the pain is not the splinter, but it could not exist without the presence of the splinter. Hope, despair, and many other experiences would be impossible if the future were not an element in our lives.

The self is a function already performed but also a function to be fulfilled, a capacity, a potentiality. Our being consists of what we have done but also of what we intend and are able to do. The past creates ability; the ability gives a sense of direction to the past. Even the capacity that was never realized, the potentiality that never had the chance of becoming actual, forms an integral part of our self.

The past and the future of the self are not, strictly speaking, separable parts; they form an indissoluble whole. The past acquires meaning in the light of the future; the future, in turn, depends upon the past. We cannot do whatever we want; our abilities depend upon our past experiences.

Some people have denied the dynamic character of the self or have relegated it to a position of secondary importance, thinking it to be incompatible with its unity. Unable to conceive of the unity of a changing being, they have considered that the process of alteration of the self only scratches its surface and that the self keeps an immutable central core. It is true that there is only one Ego for each experiential stream, but it is also true that the self is not immutable. We have seen that the self is constantly changing, that everything that happens to us enriches and modifies our self. But change does not mean substitution; rather, it means an alteration of the inner pattern. Thus, former experiences never quite disappear completely, though they can change their nature and meaning with the development of the self.

CHAPTER VII

Self and Gestalt

1. Atomism

The failure of atomistic empiricism to explain the unity and continuity of the self has led to a recrudescence of attempts to explain them on a metaempirical basis. As has been indicated, these attempts have gone astray because a primitive form of empiricism has been confused with empiricism itself and the mistakes of the former have been attributed to the latter. There is no need to take refuge in a hypothetical world which transcends experience in order to explain the unity and continuity of the self. Careful observation of experience can give us all the data necessary.

The quarrel between atomism and substantialism, as we have seen, was mainly due to the fact that each school of thought concentrated on one aspect of the self to the exclusion of the other. Because of its empirical method, atomism stressed the changing nature of the self and ignored its permanence and unity; substantialism, on the other hand, considered its permanence as of basic importance and its mutability as an accidental fact. Actually, permanence is as much a part of the nature of the self as its mutability; there is no reason why we should slight either of the two aspects. If the problem is considered empirically, we see not only that these two aspects are not incompatible but that, as a matter of fact, they are complementary: change is what gives the self stability and permanence.

Substantialism was unable to understand that the permanence and the mutability of the self were not incompatible characteristics because it conceived of the self as something simple and attributed permanence to an irreducible core and mutability to a peripheral zone. As we shall see in this chapter, such a separation does not correspond to reality. One can speak of differential zones only in a metaphorical sense, for the self is a complex unity undergoing a constant process; everything that happens to it affects, to a greater or less degree, its totality. The self is not something that can be divided in pieces but an organic, indissoluble unity.

Upon various occasions we have noted how atomistic empiricism, which became the irreconcilable enemy of substantialist rationalism, is in its root and origin closely related to such rationalism. At this point we can make a similar observation with regard to the simple nature of the self. Although atomism opposed the doctrine of the simplicity of the self it let itself be guided by this very concept in its search for the supposed primary elements which constituted it. Whenever atomism came upon a complex it did not try to comprehend it but rather made every effort to reduce it to its simple elements. Like substantialism, it believed that that which is simple, because it is irreducible and defies analysis, is somehow more real than that which can be taken to pieces. In other words, atomism transferred to the elements of the self the same qualities which substantialism had postulated with regard to the supposedly irreducible nucleus, especially the idea of something which exists by itself.[1]

This is a fact interesting not merely from the historical viewpoint, in that it discovers very intimate relations between currents which are considered to be radically opposed, but also for its present-day significance, revealing, as it does, the doctrinal basis of contemporary conceptions currently very much in vogue. And, what is more, the arguments against the supposed simplicity of the elements of the self can be applied, *mutatis mutandis*, to the simplicity of the substantial nucleus.

Let us postpone for the present a consideration of the legitimacy of the analytic procedure of atomism in order first to concentrate our attention upon the basic elements of the self, the psychic atoms.

Hume, as we know, is the founder of the atomism which is still influential at the present time. In his search for the self he comes upon perceptions, and he attributes to the latter a reality which he denies to the former because he finds "no *simplicity* in it at one time, nor *identity* in different." [2] An interpretation *contrario sensu* coincides with the general drift of the context: he attributes

1. Cf. *Treatise*, I, iv, 5 (1, 518); and above, my study of Hume, pp. 89–92.
2. *Treatise*, I, iv, 6 (1, 534).

to the perceptions the simplicity and identity which he refuses to attribute to the self.

Atomism looks upon experiences not only as something simple but also as a reality that is static, complete, separable, and able to subsist per se. When Hume speaks of his pain or his grief, his love or his hate, his perception of heat or cold, he does so as if these experiences were beyond the reach of time, fixed images upon a fixed screen. The truth of the matter is quite different. Psychic life is essentially temporal, and there is no experience without a dynamic character. This can best be seen in the processes of an emotive sort: love, hate, fear, happiness. The truly great dramatists and novelists, who often reveal a deeper knowledge of human psychology than the laboratory psychologists, have given us classic descriptions of the instability of man's emotions and the infinite variety of their development.

Even perception, which is often supposed to offer an example of great stability, undergoes constant changes. Suppose we perceive a firearm lying safely in a drawer and later we perceive the same firearm in the hands of someone who is threatening our life. Influenced by the emotive and volitive states aroused by such circumstances, the firearm may appear to us as having a different color, shape, size, etc. Perception is unstable even in simple laboratory cases, from which as far as possible all secondary states of mind have been eliminated. This is demonstrated in one of Köhler's experiments, carried out for a different purpose than that which here concerns us. I refer to his experiments on "figural after-effects," carried out in collaboration with H. Wallach[3] and based upon previous experiments made by J. J. Gibson.[4]

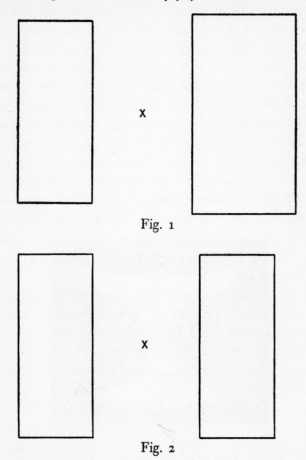

Fig. 1

Fig. 2

3. W. Köhler and H. Wallach, "Figural After-effects. An Investigation of Visual Processes," *Proceedings of the American Philosophical Society*, 88 (1944), 269–357.

4. J. J. Gibson, "Adaption, After-effect, and Contrast in the

Let us examine one of the many experiments which Köhler and Wallach report.[5] The subject observes Fig. 1 for 45 seconds at a distance of two yards. At the end of this period Fig. 1 is replaced by Fig. 2. To the subject it appears that the rectangle at the right begins to decrease in size, and the longer the period of inspection, the more marked the decrease. We shall not go into the explanations of this phenomenon; we are here concerned only with the change which the perception undergoes, despite the fact that the stimulus and other external conditions remain the same.

An even more common example may be employed to demonstrate the same instability of visual perceptions—Rubin's vase figure. If one looks at Fig. 3, normally one

Fig. 3

Perception of Curved Lines," *Journal of Experimental Psychology,* 16, 1–31.

5. Köhler and Wallach, "Figural After-effects," pp. 281–5.

sees a plain white vase; it is only after a period of fixation that the profiles of two faces spring forth. What was ground becomes figure, and figure becomes ground.

Both of these examples are merely experimental confirmations of a commonly observed fact that the atomistic psychologists ignore—the instability of perceptions and other psychic states. This constant change of the psychic states is due, in part at least, to the fact that state *b* cannot be identical to a preceding state *a* because state *b* is conditioned by, among other things, the remnant of state *a*.

It is likely that in our daily life the objects which we see are constantly changing their shapes without our noticing it, for lack of a perceptive unity of measure. Perhaps our perceptions are as unstable as our emotions. There is, at least, no doubt that their stability is not complete.

The assumed stability of our experiences explains why the atomists looked upon them as having very definite and complete reality and compared them to mosaics or Democritus' atoms. The obvious fallacy of the conception of experiences as a static reality makes it unnecessary to study the characteristics of the self derived from such a conception. The atomists manipulate experiences as a child does the pieces of a jigsaw puzzle, as if each unit were outlined with perfect distinctness and one could put the whole together and take it to pieces again merely by obeying certain mechanical laws.

Of the so-called laws which result from the supposed immutability of the elements and the permanence of the relation between them, atomistic psychologists are especially fond of the one which states that the relationship between stimulus and response is constant. Köhler and Lashley have demonstrated by experiment the error of this principle. The subject reacts to a total given situation. A chicken, for instance, in choosing between two grays, *a* and *b*, is trained to always choose the darker (*b*). When it is confronted with a new situation in which it has to choose between shade *b* and a darker one, *c*, it does not choose *b*, as is to be expected if the relationship between stimulus and response is constant, but *c*. This proves that the response depends not upon the isolated stimulus but upon the total situation. In the first case the chicken does not see shade *b* as an isolated stimulus but sees it rather as the darker of two shades offered it; in the second case, accordingly, it again chooses the darker shade, which is no longer *b* but *c*. The same experiments were done with apes, and the choice referred to the size or to the hue of objects.[6]

Experimentation and observation of facts reveal, consequently, that the changes undergone by the self do not consist of the displacement of one psychic state by another as the atomists believe. In the first place, the whole is not made up of a mere mechanical combination of the states. And in the second, these so-called states are not unities in themselves but artificial cross sections of a dynamic reality. As beautifully shown by Bergson in

6. Cf. W. Köhler, *Gestalt Psychology* (New York, Liveright, 1929), pp. 216–17.

the first pages of *Creative Evolution*, and in several other writings, they carry temporality deeply imbedded within them.

The unity of the self is not to be found in the sum of its states, for it is a unity that is dynamic and structural. At the same time, it is a matter of a continuous process and not of leaps from one state to another. It more closely resembles the flight of a bird than the hopping of a frog. Although it has its ups and downs, its accelerations and decelerations, it never stops. Its apparent discontinuity is due to the fact that we devote all our attention to its moments of culmination or to those which, for one reason or another, attract us most. These moments are like the stations at which an express train does not stop. They are important as far as the timetables are concerned, but for the traveler they are merely conventional, immobile signposts along the way.

The attitude of Hume and his present-day followers with regard to the problem of the self is similar to that of a man who would seek the structure of a cathedral in the spaces between the stones. After moving the stones one after the other and finding nothing that resembles a cathedral, he will exclaim, with the arrogance of Hume: "Where is the cathedral? Didn't I say that there was no such thing, that there were only stones and mortar?" And if one is talking to a present-day Humean, one finds it next to impossible to convince him that he has torn to pieces what he was looking for, that the cathedral cannot exist without stones but at the same time is something more than a mere heap of stones.

It is true that modern atomists do not maintain that "perceptions" are simple and that they maintain even less that they should be considered as the ultimate constituent elements. This is not due, however, to a renunciation of Hume's procedure. It is rather that they have brought this very procedure to perfection. They deny the identity and simplicity of the perceptions because they believe that these characteristics belong to elements of which perceptions are composed; they have arrived at these elements by means of a process of analysis which is merely Hume's method perfected.

Bertrand Russell, for example, gives us a demonstration of his analytical ability when he reduces psychic life to its "ultimate constituents": sensations and images. And at the very moment that the reader is beginning to tremble at the idea that artistic creation, scientific genius, and philosophic meditation are no more than variants of the combinations which result from sensations and images the author laments the fact that his analysis has come to a conclusion leaving standing two elements and not one alone, which had been his goal.[7] Does it not seem that these irreducible elements correspond in some way to substance, the final result of rationalism? And, of course, someone was bound to come along and eliminate images as well, leaving a single element: sensation. Empiricism, too, has its Spinoza.

7. Cf. Russell, *The Analysis of Mind*, chap. viii, especially pp. 144, 156.

2. *Analysis and analyticism*

A study of the validity of the procedure utilized by the atomists reveals its weaknesses even more clearly than does an analysis of the results of the procedure itself.

The analysis of psychic complexes and their reduction to supposed primary elements has no empirical justification; it makes its appearance in atomism as a presupposition which, on the face of it, has the same philosophic value as the rationalist presupposition. We are aware of the difficulties which one has to face in an attempt to eliminate all presuppositions. It is nevertheless evident that atomism has made no serious effort to justify or examine critically the procedure which it employs. It has accepted and used the procedure with no thought for its philosophic basis or for the consequences which would result from its application.

As is well known, the method that is used conditions the nature of the object under observation. If, blinded by the prestige acquired by the scientific method, we commit the stupid blunder of the modern tourist who tries to examine under the microscope a city which he is visiting for the first time, we shall not succeed in seeing the houses, the people, the plants, and the flowers. It would imply an even greater blindness to maintain that in the city there are neither houses nor people nor flowers, without realizing that they have disappeared as a consequence of the instrument chosen. The naked eye, in such a case, is a better instrument than the microscope, which, though it shows us the detail, keeps us from seeing the whole.

The analytic method has often worked like a microscope. It has revealed details which no one had ever seen before, but it has impeded our view of the whole. Again, the naked eye and the free-ranging glances of the spirit are superior to the intellect provided with the perfected technique and instruments of analysis. We need only to glance within, if we hold no prejudicial theories, to see what is hidden from the philosophers using analytic methods and blinded by the postulates of their theory and by their technique of observation.

Why should we be surprised that the wholes are not perceived if it has already been accepted in advance that analysis is the only form of apprehension? That which has been previously eliminated cannot be discovered, and it is impossible to reconstruct what should never have been destroyed.

The analytic philosophy which sprang from Hume's atomism is subject to an almost demoniac desire for destruction—destruction by reductions. When confronted by a whole, these philosophers make no effort to comprehend its nature and find the sense of the whole. They proceed immediately to chop the whole into as many parts as possible and to submit each part to the thoroughgoing test of analysis. It is like the little boy who wants to find out what makes his toy work and ends up defiantly facing a heap of loose nuts and bolts.

This destructive drive is based upon a metaphysical postulate from which another postulate, an epistemological one, is derived; these two postulates support what we might call "the fallacy of reduction." The metaphysical postulate may be stated thus: elements have a more actual reality than wholes. The epistemological consequence is obvious: the goal of philosophic knowledge is to come to grips with the basic elements which constitute reality.

From these two postulates a series of principles is derived and conditions the whole attitude of the analytic philosophers. There are two principles which particularly concern us in the study which we are making: *a*) that the "parts" or elements can be separated from the "whole" without undergoing any change; *b*) that these elements can be discovered by analysis and defined in such a way that leaves no room for doubt.

This is the theoretical apparatus which supports Russell's examination of psychic reality, for instance, in his *Analysis of Mind*. If the whole life of the spirit is reduced, ultimately, to sensations or images, how is an intellectual process distinguished from an emotion or from an act of will? Since the distinction cannot be made on the basis of constitutive element, for the only "ingredients" are sensations and images, the difference will have to be sought in the organization of these elements, in the structure which they make up together. But now we see that the only thing proved by the analytic reduction of the self is the value of the organization or structure of the elements. That is to say, it proves what it sets out to disprove. And the more extreme the analytic conclusion, the more evident the contrary thesis. If images are eliminated and everything is reduced to sensations, only the differences between the structural complexes in which these sensations are organized can explain the variety, richness, and diversity of the psychic life.

I am not proposing, of course, the abandonment of analysis as a philosophic method. It is not clear how analysis could be abandoned without falling into an attitude of contemplative mysticism, which would bring as its immediate consequence greater confusion and obscurity to the field of philosophy. What I am criticizing is *analyticism,* if we may so call it, which attempts to reduce to analysis every philosophic task and actually analyzes away what is really important.

Analysis involves the disarticulation of a complex reality whose unity is destroyed when its component members are separated. It can be used in the realm of psychic life with a great deal of profit and very little danger, provided that one is constantly aware of its limitations and consequences and never loses sight of the fact that the elements which have been separated by analysis are members of a totality which must, of necessity, remain united. Analysis should therefore be used—always, of course, keeping the totality in mind—only in order to make clear the meaning of the whole and to comprehend its inner mechanism, not in order to eliminate the whole or reduce it to a heap of disjointed pieces. Hence analysis should be applied to a structure only after the structure has been taken in and recognized as a whole; reality should not be sacrificed to the method used.

For many of the philosophers who adopt the analytic attitude, analysis is the first stage of a process, and the second stage is the reconstruction of the object analyzed.

This is the attitude which Dilthey calls "explicative" psychology, because it gives greater emphasis to the reconstructive aspect. With this he contrasts his own "descriptive and analytic" psychology.[8] But this second stage does not invalidate what has been stated concerning the first; on the contrary, the second stage is complementary to the first. So we see, for example, that the elements, even after the reconstruction, are still the most important aspect. The only thing added is the force holding the elements together, which is the association of ideas in the case of many philosophers even today. This force not only leaves intact the reality of elements but even stresses their primary importance. Likewise, the principle that the parts can be separated from the whole without undergoing any change is corroborated by the reconstructive principle that the whole is no more than the sum or the putting-together of the parts.

The analytic attitude is moreover complemented by a mechanical conception of the psychic life which tries to "explain" everything by means of simple elements and the forces that move them. When the psychic life has been put together again in this way, it has lost its organic unity, its spontaneity, its very life—all that characterizes the human being. Hence the final result seems more like a robot than a man: the parts that make it up remain unalterable, and the forces that move it are completely

8. Cf. his *Ideen über eine beschreibende und zergliedernde Psychologie, Gesammelte Schriften*, 5, 139–240. Dilthey's concept of analysis has, of course, an altogether different sense from that given it by the representatives of "analyticism."

mechanical. The process of reconstruction cannot give us what analysis has previously destroyed—the organic coherence of the inner life. Reconstruction is neither necessary nor possible, for this organic unity is a primary reality and not the conclusion of a system.

3. The concept of Gestalt

What is the self before its unity has been broken down by analysis? In what does its organic or structural unity consist?

Let us first make clear that this unity is not one that transcends the empirical world, the world of experiences. It is a unity derived from the very experiences themselves. There is nothing under or above the totality of experiences. If one overlooks the word "totality" or interprets it in an atomistic sense, this statement would be equivalent of subscribing to Hume's theory. But we should never interpret the totality or structure of experiences as a mere sum or aggregate of the same. The experiential totality has qualities which are not possessed by the members which constitute it. Consequently the characteristics of the total structure of the self cannot be deduced, necessarily, from the characteristics of each of the experiences taken separately.

It may perhaps come as a surprise that one should attribute to the whole certain qualities not possessed by the parts which constitute it, but only a person who subscribes dogmatically to the atomistic theory and refuses to accept empirical evidence against this theory will be surprised. I refer to the evidence collected in more than

30 years of work by one of the most fruitful schools of contemporary psychology, the *Gestaltpsychologie*.[9]

Some simple concrete examples will demonstrate the impossibility of explaining certain wholes by means of the elements which constitute them and will show that in the case of structures the whole comes to take on properties not possessed by the constituent parts.

Observe, for example, the following melody:

Fig. 4

9. Some representatives of analytical philosophy seem to accept the conclusions of the *Gestalttheorie,* but they persist in retaining their analytical principles; the two attitudes seem to me to be mutually exclusive.

Russell, for example, writes: "*Mental phenomena, like all other phenomena, consist of particulars variously related.* Sensations and images are merely names for these particulars, sensations being those which have proximate causes outside the brain, and images being all the rest. I have no objection whatever to *Gestalt* psychology, and I am not the least anxious to deny that *wholes have important properties not necessarily deducible from their constituents and the relations among these.* I refuse, however, to be in any way humble about the fact that my psychology is not yet adequate to explain the most complex of the higher mental processes. One might as well complain of Galileo because he did not understand electricity. *The proper scientific procedure is always to master the simplest phenomena first.*" Italics mine. This passage is part of a reformulation of his ideas written by B. Russell in June of 1931 for Charles W. Morris', *Six Theories of Mind* (Chicago, University of Chicago Press, 1932); cf. p. 137.

Let us now transpose this melody from B-flat major to
C major. The same melody will be recognized at once,
although the eight notes which constitute it have been
changed.

Fig. 5

One can, of course, give many examples of structure
without having recourse to those offered by the Gestaltpsychologie. A typical case, perhaps, is that of a word, a
sentence, or a book. A written word, such as "revolution,"
has a meaning and a great variety of connotations for
which it would be vain to seek in the letters that form it.
It is also possible, using the same letters, to form other
words, which have another meaning or lack meaning altogether. What is more, sometimes the word does not
in itself have a single unequivocal meaning; it must be
placed in a context—a structure—in order to acquire
one. Thus, the word "revolution" would have a different
meaning according to whether it refers to the revolutions
of an airplane's propeller or to the revolutions in Central
America. Letters, which are the elements that constitute
a written word, tell us nothing concerning their meanings.
It is evident that words have properties which cannot be
found in letters, and sentences have properties which cannot be found in words. Aristotle was right when he stated
that tragedy and comedy are written with the same alpha-

bet and yet, in their significance, are completely different.

Even if one considers words in isolation, he will notice that many allude to a structure of which they form parts —for example, side, near, part, hole, left, etc. In general, this is true of those words which denote a relationship, in the ordinary sense of the term; but it is not an exclusive property of such words, as may be seen in "hole," for instance.[1]

Although antecedents of the Gestalttheorie may be unearthed in modern thought,[2] and even in ancient philosophy,[3] this concept has acquired great significance and fruitfulness in contemporary philosophy. Christian Ehrenfels is recognized as the most immediate forerunner. In 1890 Ehrenfels published an article entitled "Über Gestaltqualitäten" in a little-known review called *Vierteljahrschrift für wissenschaftliche Philosophie*.[4] Ehrenfels, who

1. Cf. Köhler, *Gestalt Psychology*, pp. 221–3.

2. Goethe, for example, used this term, especially with regard to the natural sciences, in the same sense in which the Gestalttheorie uses it at the present time. Cf. *ibid.*, p. 192.

3. Plato writes in his *Theaetetus* that *all* and the *whole* are not the same thing (204^b), and farther on (204^e) that "the whole does not consist of parts, for if it consisted of all the parts it would be the all." Aristotle made similar statements, especially in the *Metaphysics*. In his *Gestalt Psychology* (New York, 1935), George W. Hartmann (p. 9 n. 7) calls attention to a statement by the Chinese sage Lao-tse (B.C. 600), who states in his *Tao-tê-ching*, 39th. that "the sum of the parts is not the whole."

4. 14, No. 3, 249–92. It was later reprinted, with commentaries, as a monograph with the title, *Das Primzahlengesetz entwickelt und dargestellt auf Grund der Gestalttheorie* (Leipzig, 1922).

took E. Mach's work, *Die Analyse der Empfindungen*, as his point of departure, characterized structural quality (*Gestaltqualität*) as "something that belongs to a psychic complex but to none of its constituents, and persists even when transposed." Four years later, in 1894, W. Dilthey developed the concept of structure in his work entitled *Ideas Concerning a Descriptive and Analytic Psychology*. Many other German philosophers and psychologists [5] have taken the concept of structure as a basis for investigation; one should mention in particular Felix Krueger and his teacher Hans Cornelius.[6] But the concept of Gestalt is at present associated with the psychological school initiated by Max Wertheimer and developed by him and his students, Kurt Koffka and Wolfgang Köhler, first in Germany and then in the United States.[7]

5. The English-speaking world has always been inclined toward atomism and, even after the three great proponents of the Gestalttheorie have established themselves in the United States, continues to look with distrust upon a concept which it considers to be "metaphysical" and not scientific. Even so, in the past century, Stout in his *Analytical Psychology* (1896), 1, chap. iii, raised problems with reference to structure in the field of perception.

6. For an outline of the antecedents of the theory of Gestalt, see Madison Bentley's article, "Psychology of Mental Arrangement," *American Journal of Psychology*, 12 (1902), 269–93.

7. In a less specific sense, there are a great many contemporary philosophers who have emphasized the structural aspect of reality. Bergson's classic attack upon atomism is based on the conception of structure. And Whitehead writes in *Science and the Modern World* (Cambridge, 1926), p. 145, that science "is becoming the study of organisms. Biology is the study of the larger organisms; whereas physics is the study of the smaller organisms."

The Gestaltpsychologie was first known to the public through the work of Wertheimer on the perception of apparent motion.[8] Koffka describes, in the following terms, the situation which Wertheimer had to face and overcome:

> The dilemma of psychology, then, was this: on the one hand it was in possession of explanatory principles in the scientific sense, but these principles did not solve the most important problems of psychology, which therefore remained outside its scope; on the other hand, it dealt with these very problems, but without scientific explanatory principles; *to understand* took the place of *to explain*.

> This dilemma must have been prominent in Wertheimer's mind even when he was a student. Perceiving the merits and faults of both sides, he could not join either, but he had to try to find a solution of this acute crisis. In this solution two principles could not be sacrificed: the principles of science and of

---

And he has written before that "an electron within a living body is different from an electron outside it, by reason of the plan of the body." *Ibid.*, p. 111.

Koffka recognizes his affinity with Whitehead in his article upon the Gestalt in the *Encyclopedia of the Social Sciences*. Köhler maintains that M. Planck's lecture on "The Present Situation of Theoretical Physics" contains the first clear recognition of the principle of the Gestalt in the natural sciences.

8. Wertheimer, "Experimentelle Studien über das Sehen von Bewegung," *Zeitschrift für Psychologie*, 61 (1912), 161–265, reprinted in the volume entitled *Drei Abhandlungen zur Gestalttheorie* (Erlangen, 1925).

meaning. And yet these very two were the origin of the whole difficulty. Scientific progress occurs very often by a re-examination of the fundamental scientific concepts. And to such a re-examination Wertheimer devoted his efforts.[9]

Very soon the Gestalttheorie acquired great prestige in Germany and sometime afterward became one of the most fruitful schools of contemporary psychology. It was first applied to the field of perception and then extended to the study of memory, the process of learning, and personality.[1] Although at first the Gestaltists used the concept of Gestalt in the field of experimental psychology and in relation to very concrete problems, they did not conceal their belief that it was a concept that could be applied to many other fields [2] and that it would bring a veritable revolution to the world of philosophy.[3] Koffka seemed to be

9. Cf. K. Koffka, *Principles of Gestalt Psychology* (New York, Harcourt, Brace, 1935), p. 20.

1. The literature on Gestalt psychology has become very extensive; it is scattered in works written in five or six different languages and in numerous articles appearing in psychological reviews. Of all these reviews, the *Psychologische Forschung*, official organ of the movement since 1922, was the one that offered the material of most interest.

2. Köhler demonstrated the existence of physical Gestalten in his work on *Die physischen Gestalten in Ruhe und im stationärem Zustand* (Braunschweig, 1920).

3. The latest word in Gestalt psychology is Kurt Lewin's "topology." (He was formerly Köhler's aid in Berlin but established himself in the United States as a refugee from Nazi racial persecution.) Cf. his *Principles of Topological Psychology* (Lon-

expressing the consensus of his fellow workers when he wrote in 1931: "The term Gestalt is a short name for a category of thought comparable to other general categories like substance, causality, function. But Gestalt may be considered more than simply an addition to pre-existing conceptual principles; its generality is so great that one is forced to ask whether causality itself or substance does not fall legitimately under it." [4]

So far we have stated only that the self is a structure and have referred briefly to the antecedents of the Gestalt theory. We need now to examine the concept of Gestalt in order to show how it may be applied to the self.

What is it that characterizes a Gestalt? Like any other fundamental concept, that of Gestalt presents a degree of complexity which does not allow one to enunciate in a few words all the richness of its content.[5] Nevertheless, there

---

don and New York, McGraw-Hill, 1936) and his A Dynamic Theory of Personality (London and New York, McGraw-Hill, 1935).

4. K. Koffka, "Gestalt," Encyclopedia of the Social Sciences, ed. E. R. A. Seligman (New York, Macmillan, 1931), 6, 642.

5. It is a notable fact that in all the extensive bibliography on the Gestalttheorie there are few worth-while studies of the Gestalt concept itself. Perhaps this is due to the fact that the theory arose as the result of concrete psychological investigations and that those who advocated it did not want to appear to be "metaphysicians." Cf. Koffka, Principles of Gestalt Psychology, p. 683.

The briefest and best work that I know of on the concept of Gestalt is Wertheimer's article, "Gestalt Theory," Social Research, 11, No. 1 (Feb. 1944), which is a version of a lecture given in Berlin in 1924. Of the three original proponents of the movement, Wertheimer seems to be the one who has the greatest in-are certain characteristics which seem to be fundamental. First, there is the one that has already been emphasized: a structural whole—a Gestalt—has qualities not possessed by any of the elements which form it. In this sense, a Gestalt or structure is set in contrast with a mere sum of elements. The physical and chemical qualities of a cubic yard of water are the same as those of each gallon that makes it up. The whole, in this case, is no more than the mere sum of its parts. In the case of a structure, on the other hand, this is not so, as we have seen in considering the character of a melody; it possesses qualities which cannot be found in any of the notes, for it can be transposed without being changed into another melody.

The above-mentioned characteristic does not mean, of course, that a Gestalt is completely independent of the members which constitute it. In the first place, there can be no structure without members. But the dependence of structure upon members does not stop here—the removal, addition, or fundamental alteration of a member modifies the whole structure, as can be seen in the case of an organism.[6] Any important alteration or suppression of a member alters the totality of an organism and may even

terest and ability with regard to philosophy. Koffka devotes less than one page (pp. 682-3) to an examination of the concept of Gestalt in his *Principles of Gestalt Psychology*. Chap. vi of Köhler's *Gestalt Psychology*, which promises to expound the theory of the concept, actually restricts itself to the examination of concrete problems of the psychology of perception.

6. Lewin defines a Gestalt in his *Principles of Topological Psychology* (p. 208) as a "system whose parts are dynamically connected in such a way that a change of one part results in a change of all the other parts."

cause its disappearance. This does not happen in the case of a sum. We can remove one, two, thirty, or forty gallons of water without causing the rest to undergo any important change in quality.

But not only does the structural whole suffer alteration when one of its members is taken away, the member that is taken away is also basically altered. A hand separated from the body is unable to feel or to seize an object—it ceases to be a hand—whereas the gallon of water separated from the rest retains practically all of its properties. This characteristic, taken along with the foregoing one, will suffice for the definition of a member of a structure. A member of a structure is that which cannot be removed without affecting the whole structure and losing its own nature when separated from the "whole." Conversely, we can characterize the "mere sum" as something made up of "parts" or "elements" that undergo no change when joined to other "parts" and which can be removed without producing any change either in itself or in what remains. The relationship between the parts is that of mere juxtaposition.

The difference between structure and mere sum does not stem solely from the fact that the parts of the latter are independent of the whole and that the members of the former are conditioned by the structure. There is also the fact that the parts may be homogeneous, whereas the members must offer diversity and even opposition of characteristics. One gallon of water is just as much water as any other gallon or measure. The same is true of one brick in a pile of bricks or of each grain of sand in the desert.

On the contrary, in an organism each member has its own specific nature—the heart is the heart and cannot perform the functions of the liver or kidneys. There is not only diversity among the members but also opposition; and this opposition is subsumed into the unity which organizes them. The unification and organization of the members which make up a structure do not come about at the expense of the peculiar and distinctive qualities of each member. Organization is not the equivalent of homogenization, and unity does not contradict the multiplicity and diversity of the elements. This multiplicity and diversity must always be maintained as absolutely essential. Thus we find structure to be the result of a dialectic play of opposites, of a struggle between the members; it seems to hang by the thread which establishes a dynamic balance. But this unity is not of an abstract sort. A concept which organizes different members into a unity by grouping them in agreement with a common note does not constitute a structure. One essential aspect of the structure is lacking: its unity must be concrete. For that reason I use the term "structure" rather than "form" or "configuration" to translate the German word Gestalt, which, besides carrying the connotation of these two latter concepts, designates a unity that is *concrete*.[7]

4. *The structural unity of the self*

When we considered the applicability of the category of substance to the self, we noticed that none of the three classic characteristics of this concept—immutability, sim-

7. Cf. Köhler, *Gestalt Psychology*, p. 192.

plicity, and independence—belonged to the self. We obtained a similarly negative result from the consideration of the atomistic conception. In the first place, the supposed psychic atom is a poorly defined unit which, when one attempts to fix it with any precision, vanishes into thin air, becoming a mere arbitrary instant in an uninterrupted process. In the second place, the aggregation of atoms, which can have only a relationship of juxtaposition one to another, looks like a grotesque caricature of the real organic unity of the self. Let us now see if the category which we have called Gestalt or structure is any more successful.[8]

It seems unquestionable that the psychic life is not chaotic, that each state or experience is connected to all

8. An exposition of the Gestalt theory of the Ego may be found in Koffka's work, *Principles of Gestalt Psychology*, especially pp. 319–42. If one compares Koffka's theory with the one which I am here proposing, he will see that although I have taken the concept of structure from the Gestalttheorie I am not subscribing to the theory of the German psychologist. In the first place, Koffka defines psychology as the science of behavior (*ibid.*, p. 25)—though not in Watson's sense of the word—and faces the problem of the self or Ego as a problem of *segregation* from its field (pp. 319–33). The procedure that I am following is just the reverse: my problem is that of the *integration*. This fundamental difference in our points of departure and the philosophical attitude which I have adopted (which obliges me to transcend the limits of experimental psychology, a thing which Koffka never does since he has adopted a strictly scientific attitude) allow me more freedom in my thesis. What is more, in my opinion the categories of function, process, and intentionality are just as important as that of structure in the interpretation of the self.

the rest. This connection, however, is not of experience to experience, like the links of a chain, for if this were so there would be a fixed order of connections and in order to get to one link we should necessarily have to go by way of the preceding ones. But in the same way that Köhler showed that there is no constant relation between stimulus and response, it would be easy to show that in like manner there is no constant relation between one experience and another. No laboratory experiment is needed to prove this, for our daily experiences supply all the material we require—the sound and sight of the sea is exhilarating one day and depressing the next; the same piece of music arouses in us different reactions according to the situation in which we hear it; our arrival at the same port and in the same ship can start altogether different trains of reflection in us, depending on whether we have arrived to stay for the rest of our life or only for a short vacation; the memory of a disagreement with a friend, which irritated us so much when it happened, may now provoke only an indifferent smile. The relations of experiences to each other resemble the relations between stimuli and responses in the fact that they arise within a given context.

These undeniable data of the psychic life are founded on the fact that the self is not a sum of experiences or an aggregate of parts in juxtaposition but a structure—in the sense defined above; whatever happens to one of its elements affects the whole, and the whole in turn exerts an influence upon each element. It is because the whole reacts as a structural unity and not as a mechanism that a stimulus can provoke consequences in an altogether different field from the one in which it has arisen. Thus, a strictly intellectual problem can give rise to emotional torment, and a fact of an emotional sort can have far-reaching volitional consequences. The self is not departmentalized —like modern bureaucracy—but constitutes an organic unity with intimate, complex, and varied interrelations.

The self presents itself, then, as an organized whole, an integrated structure, and experiences are related to one another not through but within the whole. For that reason, when the structure is modified the nature of the experiences and of the relationships between them are also modified. The interdependence of the different experiential groups shows that the self is a structure which is organized and "makes sense" and that each member occupies its proper place within the structure.

This does not mean, of course, that the structure which constitutes the self cannot be analyzed and broken down, theoretically, into less complex structures. It does mean, however, that we are in fact dealing with a unity that is formed upon substructures and the intimate and complex interrelation of these substructures.[9]

And here we notice another characteristic of the concept of structure which is directly applicable to the self: the members of a structure are heterogeneous in contrast with the homogeneity of the parts of a nonstructural unity. Let us state, first of all, that the structure which constitutes the self, being a very complex structure, is

9. By substructure I mean any of the structural parts that constitute the total Gestalt that makes up the self.

made up not of "simple members" but of substructures; it is consequently to the heterogeneity of these substructures that we are referring. It must also be kept in mind that the substructures are not of an abstract nature, like concepts, and that we are not trying to reconstruct a reality by juxtaposing abstractions such as the so-called "faculties of the soul."

The complexity and heterogeneity of the structure are twofold: on the one hand there is the complexity which we may call transversal; on the other there is the horizontal or, better, the temporal complexity. In actuality the self embraces the combination of both complexes, which do not and cannot exist in separation.

If we make a cross section at a given moment in our life, we find that we have a slice of a process that is made up of bundles of three different kinds of experience: the intellectual, the emotive, and the volitive. This shows that not even in the briefest moment of our life is it possible to catch ourselves concentrated upon a single type of experience. To prove this statement it is necessary to show that every experiential situation, however elemental it may be—provided that it is real—is made up of intellectual, emotive, and volitive elements.

Let us begin with the emotive elements. Every perception or representation is accompanied by an emotive reaction. What happens is that the reaction, in general, is very weak and passes unnoticed. Let us leave out of consideration those special perceptions which produce a pleasure or pain which is so intense that no one would dare deny the existence of the relation: the taste of something sweet or savory, on the one hand, or a deep burn or cut, on the other. Let us, rather, consider the perceptions of color, which are generally held to possess a weaker affective tonality. We are walking in the country just as the sun is about to go down behind the horizon. Without being in anguish, we feel a certain sadness in our spirit. Suddenly we realize that we are still wearing a pair of dark glasses. We take them off, and at once a glow of happiness surges through our spirit. With the change of the color of the landscape there is a change in affective tonality. This is a phenomenon known not only to psychologists but also to housewives, who change the color of the wallpaper because it is "sad" or remove heavy curtains so that happiness may come in with the sunlight. The common expressions of "sad color" and "gay color" have been coined to express the bonds of affective tonality which tend to be attached to visual perceptions. We have been concerned solely with perceptions of color, but what we have discovered could be applied equally well to the other forms of visual perception, as well as to auditive and other kinds of perceptions.

For reasons of clarity we have restricted our attention to the affective tonality which accompanies perceptions, but in all of the examples cited there are also volitional elements. When we noticed that the sadness of the landscape was due in part to the dark tint of our spectacles, we ceased to use them for the rest of that day; similarly, on the following day, if the intensity of the sunlight irritated us, we should decide to put them on again. The housewife does the same thing in the cases alluded to, and we repeat the process daily when we draw nearer to that which arouses in us a certain pleasure and draw away from that which displeases us.

We have referred to the volitive act which has its origin in an emotive state, but the order can be just the reverse. A resolution that we make—or the lack of resolution, which is also a case of volition—may have an agreeable or disagreeable effect upon us, according to the circumstances. We are never left in a state of absolute indifference. Perceptions and images, too, are accompanied by a volitional state, though at times only in its most elemental forms. An object attracts our attention, and we direct our gaze toward it. We approach, we withdraw, we choose between two or more alternatives. Total volitional indifference toward something we perceive or imagine seems to be as impossible as total emotive indifference.

In order to prove that the three different states are always present in each cross section of our psychic life, we now have only to show that "intellectual" experiences (perceptions, images, and the like) cannot be absent when we undergo emotional and volitional experiences. But is it possible that we can be afraid or happy without having any sort of perception or images? It does not seem possible. An image is present in the case of a person who is frightened by phantoms as well as in the case of a person who sees a real danger approaching him. And what has been said with respect to fear or happiness can be applied to the other emotive states. In the same way that there is no perception or image that is not accompanied by an emotive tonality, it seems impossible that there could be an emotion simultaneous with a complete absence of an image.

The same thing happens with regard to volition, for we do not make resolutions out of thin air—a resolution presupposes a definite situation. And this situation must occur in a perceptive, imaginative, or conceptual form. There is, therefore, no volitional experience that is unaccompanied by an intellectual one.

So far we have arrived only at an idea of the "transversal" structure of our psychic life. This is inadequate, of course, for our life is a process, and any cross section implies its paralyzation. Nevertheless, such an approach is very useful, for the "longitudinal" structure cannot be understood if one does not first have a transversal idea of each of the bundles that make it up.

Atomism was unable to comprehend either the transversal substructure of our self or the substructure which we might call longitudinal. Under the misconception that a whole is constituted necessarily by the sum or mechanical aggregate of the parts, it ignored the complex inner relationships which make it impossible to explain the structure of the self by the application of the physical principle of causality.

The atomists should not be blamed too much for their failure to perceive the structure that goes through time, its development and evolution. Their error in this case is due to their conception of time as an empty and indifferent form which may be filled by either one content or another, without making any difference. Psychological time, however, is not empty, and it is impossible to separate its content from its form. It cannot be disintegrated into the supposed instants which constitute it, for each psychological "moment" is a structure with unity of meaning. And, what is more, the "present" conceived of by the atomists is arbitrary. It aspires to be a fragment without extension. But for the present to make real sense it must contain the past and the future.

The gradual change of structure through time can be seen both by observing the development of the process itself and by comparing cross sections made at different points in the process. If one makes such a comparison, one will notice not only that the experiences vary but also that the type of structure does. At one moment the emotive is predominant and the intellectual and volitional are secondary; at another the intellectual is predominant, etc. The only thing that remains is the presence of a structure made up of three types of experiences.

This diversity and opposition among the elements which constitute the self should not lead us to forget the unity which characterizes every structure. The self is no exception. Its multiplicity does not exclude its unity or vice versa. And this is not the abstract unity of a concept which points to what is common; it is a concrete unity, of "flesh and blood" as Unamuno would say, for there is nothing more real and concrete than our self. Diversity underlies the structure but is in turn lost within it, for the elements uphold each other mutually in an intimate sort of interweaving in which it is impossible to distinguish warp from woof. This is not because the three types of substructure have equivalent strength and no one of them dominates the other two—as in the theory of the so-called balance of power—but because they vary constantly. At a given moment one element stands forth as the figure and the others form the ground; after a while there is a change of roles. These changes are explained by the fact that the self is a dynamic structure and thus resembles a symphony rather than a painting.

We should perhaps stress the point that the changes undergone by the self are not due exclusively to a different distribution of the members, for the members themselves are of a dynamic nature. Moreover, the self is constituted not only of members but also of the *tensions* produced by the reciprocal play of influences. The breakdown of the equilibrium of tensions is what generally produces the most important changes.

It now appears obvious that the relations between the experiences are not fixed, for each experience as it is incorporated into the structure modifies its former state. This member in turn undergoes the influence of the whole, which is another characteristic of a Gestalt easy to find in the self. Thus, the perceptions which we have at this moment depend upon our former state. The new experience immediately acquires the coloration given it both by the basic structure of the self and by the particular situation in which it finds itself at that moment. If we are happy and in pleasant company, for example, the color of the spectacles we happen to be wearing has very little effect upon the emotive state of our spirit. This is not because visual perception ceases to have emotional tonality but because a greater affective tone—the happiness which results from a different cause—completely over-shadows it. What is more, the stable nature of the self colors the transitory state. There are people who give the impression of seeing the world in the rosiest colors, what-ever the tint of the spectacles they wear, and there are others who see clouds in the clearest sky.

This is the influence of the whole upon the member which is incorporated, but there is also an influence of the member upon the whole. We must not forget that a struc-ture is not suspended in thin air but rests solely upon the members which constitute it. A symphonic orchestra is something more than the sum of the musicians that go to form it, but it cannot exist without the musicians. A self without the experiential structures that go to make it up would be the same as an orchestra without musicians, that is, a pure fantasy, the fantasy of a spiritual entity that would be unable to love, hate, decide, want, perceive, etc., and would pretend to be immutable substance. Such a concept would be immutable without doubt, but it would have the immutability of nothingness.

In the same way that the total suppression of the ex-periential structures would mean the suppression of the self, any change or alteration of a member has repercus-sions on the whole structure. By this I do not mean a man lacking in emotional life, for example, for it is obvious that he would not be a man but a mere caricature, or pro-jection on a plane of two dimensions, of a three-dimen-sional reality. I am referring to the alteration of a structural subcomplex. Abulia, for example, is a disease of the will, but the changes which it provokes are not limited to the volitional—it has immediate repercussions in the emotive and intellectual spheres and consequently in the total structure. Its intellectual repercussions are easily seen, for the person suffering from abulia is unable to concentrate his attention, and thus his intellectual processes break down completely. And the emotional sphere is impaired too, for the sufferer is unable, by an act of the will, to get rid of the emotion which has taken control of him, so he lets himself be so possessed by this emotion that it changes his whole personality.

Of the characteristics of the structure that are applicable to the self we have only to consider now the first and most important, that is, the fact that the structure possesses qualities not possessed by the members that make it up. At this stage in our inquiry it seems a waste of time to insist that this is one of the characteristics of the self. Let us consider only the most obvious reasons. The self has a permanence—in the sense of constant presence—and a stability that the experiences and experiential groups do not have. Experiences are totally unstable; transiency is their characteristic. The self, on the other hand, remains stable in the face of the coming and going of experiences. If experiences do not have stability, even less can they have permanence, which is the fundamental characteristic of the self. And this is not all. The structure of the self is such that the members that make it up cannot exist in separation from it. There is no experience that does not belong to a particular self. The self depends, then, upon the experiences, but it is not equivalent to their sum. It is a structural quality.

When we state that the self is a structure, we do not maintain that everything that happens to us automatically occupies the position in the totality that belongs to it, as if it were a matter of a sort of "pre-established harmony." There are facts that have no major significance for us, that come in like so much dead matter—even though, under certain circumstances, the accumulation of such matter can acquire significance.[1]

The use of an interpretative category does not mean that all the facts are organized in accord with the category; only those are which have significance. Thus, when the scientist states that natural phenomena are related by causality, he does not claim that all, but only certain, facts are connected to others by the relation of cause and effect. In addition to this relation there are many others, such as that of proximity in time and in space, etc., but they are not so important as causality for the comprehension and explanation of reality. The same thing happens with regard to structure—it is a concept that, in my opinion, better than any other reveals the intimate nature of the self, but it is not applicable to everything that happens to the self.

That the self has a structural unity is proved not only by the reasons given so far but also by certain very concrete experiments, of which I shall cite only one, the ex-

1. The slamming of a door, for example, is a trivial fact that has little meaning. Nevertheless, if we should listen for a period of ten hours or so to such slamming at a fairly rapid rate, it could very well give rise to a profound psychological disturbance in us and in this way affect the totality of our self.

periment carried out by Arnheim, one of Wertheimer's pupils at the University of Berlin.[2] Arnheim asked his subjects to match different aspects or expressions of certain well-known personages. Sometimes the experiment involved deciding to which person—Leonardo, Michelangelo, or Raphael—a page of manuscript belonged; sometimes it involved matching up persons, whose pictures were shown, with their handwriting, a characteristic page of their works, or descriptions of the ways in which they were wont to behave. The percentage of correct answers was so high that it would be absurd to attribute them to mere chance.

The experiment proves that the different aspects of a personality and all its forms of expression proceed from a unified structure and they are therefore harmonious among themselves. This fact was already pointed out by Johann K. Lavater in his work, published in four volumes in 1775–78, entitled *Physiognomische Fragmente zur Beförderung der Menschenkenntnis und Menschenliebe.*

It is clear that not all the aspects of a personality are equally important; otherwise we need to know only one feature to grasp the whole structure. Besides, the relation among the different features is very complex and therefore the "axis" of a personality is not easy to discover.

2. Referred to by Koffka, *Principles of Gestalt Psychology,* p. 678. See also G. W. Allport, *Personality. A Psychological Interpretation* (London, 1949), pp. 476–81; G. W. Allport and P. E. Vernon, *Studies in Expressive Movement* (New York, 1933), *passim;* and P. E. Vernon's article in *Psychol. Bull.,* 33 (1936), 149–77.

Every day we come across examples of definite personal structure. Among criminals, for example, a certain individual is capable of killing a child but is incapable of stealing a brief case from a careless person on a streetcar. He has a certain professional pride which derives from his "personal style." The police know it. When a crime is committed, the police analyze its characteristics and look for the probable criminal within a file arranged according to the personal style of each criminal.

In the same way, a person knowing the people who run a political party, a business company, or a nation can tell who is the author of a certain platform, policy, or decree. The style reveals the author and identifies him. On the same level of comparison, a careful study discloses the affinities that exist between a predilection for a certain type of music and an inclination toward a particular kind of painting or poetry. It would seem that the arts were organized in certain structural unities that correspond to certain psychological structures.

Sometimes the structure appears to be fragmentary, and it is difficult to determine in a concrete case. This difficulty, in the majority of cases, is due to the fact that the structure is not well defined and presents contours which are hard to discern; this is the situation of the so-called "man without personality." His typical structure is actually characterized by its very vagueness.

In cases in which the structure seems to be fragmentary —as, for example, a man who is "revolutionary" in politics and "reactionary" in science or vice versa—one should not judge too hastily. In the first place, concepts like "revolutionary" and "reactionary" are very ambiguous, and the two terms may mean completely different things in science and politics. In the second place, one should not underestimate the different motives that interfere with an attitude, however scientific this attitude may seem: personal situations, resentments, sympathies, etc. These difficulties do not invalidate the doctrine but rather emphasize the complexity of the self and serve as a warning that one must be very careful not to fall into simplistic interpretations.

5. Problems solved by the structural conception [3]

A. PERMANENCE AND MUTABILITY OF THE SELF. At the beginning of this chapter we saw that both substantialism and atomism were unable to give an adequate picture of the self because they could not comprehend how its permanence and continuity could be compatible with the changes that it undergoes. Substantialism emphasized the permanence and atomism the mutability.

The structural conception that we are here proposing allows us to see that the two characteristics are not only compatible but also complementary. The historical survey of past thought on the subject, which occupied the first part of this book, showed us that substantialism could not understand the changing nature of the self because it held fast to an irreducible and immutable nucleus and that Hume's atomism, in its effort to destroy the doctrine

3. What follows should be regarded as an illustration of the doctrine of the self as a functional Gestalt.

of a substantial nucleus, confused it with the very real permanence and continuity of the self.

If we free ourselves of the limitations of both historical positions and observe reality just as it presents itself, we shall see that the permanence and continuity of the self are based upon its structural character, for it is a dynamic structure made up not only of the elements which we can isolate in a cross section of our life but also of the substructures that form the complex longitudinal bundles that constitute the self. And change occurs each time a new element is taken in, which alters but does not destroy the structure.

In this way the constant alteration of the self insures its stability. It is undeniable that a new experience modifies, or can modify, the structure of the self. The loss of a child or a friend, a war, a religious experience, etc. can produce such an inner commotion that they may alter the total structure. From that time on we are not the same person as before. We act in a different way, we see life in a different perspective, and it may be that not only the future but also the past is colored by the new attitude. But it is just this experience causing us to change which gives endurance to the self. From now on we shall be the man who has lost his son or his friend or who had this or that religious experience. Other children that we may have or the new friends which we may take into our hearts may cover up but can never completely obliterate the existence of an experience that at one time shook us deeply and persists in the structure of our spirit despite all that may happen to us in the future.

What happens on a large scale in the case of experiences that are profoundly moving happens on a smaller scale in all the other experiences of our life. Each new experience alters the structure or substructure to which it is connected, and thus it is incorporated "definitively," so to speak. Whatever happens afterward may alter the meaning of the experience within the whole—increasing it or diminishing it—but it can never erase the experience completely.

An analogy of a physical sort, even though inadequate to characterize our psychic life, may perhaps make clear the meaning of what I am trying to put across. The self resembles, in this respect, a mixture of colors. If we add to the mixture a new color—for example, blue—the mixture will be altered to a degree that will depend upon the quantity and shade of blue added and upon the combination of colors that were there before. This quantity of blue which produces a change in the former mixture is incorporated definitively into the whole, and however many more colors we add we shall never be able completely to counteract its presence.

The nature of the whole and the influence of the element incorporated into it are controlled, in the case of the analogy, by certain stable physical laws in which quantity plays an important role. This is not the case with psychic structures, in which quantity gives way to equality. Psychic structures obey certain principles, carefully studied by the Gestalt psychologists in the case of visual perception, which also exist in all the other orders of life and in the constitution of the total structure of the self.

These general principles governing the organization of our total personality are what the most psychologically acute educators use as the basis for their choice of one type of experience rather than another in their endeavor to devise a system of corrective education for an aberrant personality.

Every self has a center or axis around which its structure is organized. When the personality has already developed, this axis is what gives direction and organization to our life, not only in that new experiences do not succeed in dislodging it from its route but also in that it chooses the type of experience that it finds to be in tune with it. But it is not a nucleus immutable in itself or fixed in relation to the rest of the structure. In the first place it undergoes an evolution which we can consider normal. The axis that predominates changes at the different stages of our life. In our earliest childhood the predominant experiential substructure is that related to alimentation, later it is play, and so on through life.

What is more, the center undergoes sudden displacements caused by new experiences that shake and modify the total structure. This is the case with the soldier who, according to war records, after devoting his life to the acquisition or intensification of his capacity for destruction and after exercising this capacity for years at the cost of many lives, suddenly discovers "the truth," "finds himself," decides that "we are all brothers." The center of his personality is completely displaced. His technical capacity as a killer, in which he formerly took pride—and centered his whole personality—is now a source of humiliation and shame. His personality must retrace its steps and choose another route.

These changes are due to many varied and complex reasons. Usually they have a long period of germination, as it were, in the world of the subconscious and burst forth full blown at a propitious moment. I recall the case of an American pilot who fought for several years in the Pacific; all of a sudden "the truth was revealed to him" while he was reading, more or less by chance, certain passages in the Bible. At other times the change comes about because of the intensification of the means of destruction; the explosion of the atomic bomb produced a psychological shock in many of those who had launched 200-pound bombs under the same flag. Most commonly it comes about because of the shock of contrast; the soldier, in the midst of hatred, destruction, and death, comes across people who are devoting their lives to healing, in a spirit of disinterested love, the physical and moral wounds that other men cause. These external situations usually act as the immediate cause for the eruption of subterranean currents; at other times they stir up for the first time currents that burst forth later on, if a propitious situation presents itself.

We should not be surprised that an apparently insignificant fact may be able to change the total structure of our personality after it has been stable for many years; in the psychological realm quantities are of no great importance. The principle, *causa aequat effectum*, is not valid in the interrelations of the different elements. Gestalt psychology has shown us how the constitution of the structure and its alteration are governed by principles that have nothing to do with the principle of causality in its simplistic interpretation as the equal of cause and effect. An example of organization in the field of visual perception can make clear the meaning of what I am saying. If we draw these three lines (Fig. 6), we see not three lines but a structure that we call a triangle. Let us add another line; it is still the same structure. We continue to see a triangle with a meaningless line inside (Fig. 7). Let us add another line; the structure remains (Fig. 8). But if we add two new lines, similar to the previous ones, we see the breakdown of the former structure and the appearance of a new one. We have ceased to see a triangle with certain meaningless lines inside and now see a face (Fig. 9).

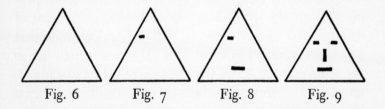

Fig. 6   Fig. 7   Fig. 8   Fig. 9

In general, the modifications produced by new experiences affect the total structure only indirectly and to a small degree, for they only modify a substructure whose alteration is not sufficiently important to change the total structure. This fact has been well observed in the field of visual perception. Wertheimer has shown that considerable changes can be introduced without altering a perceptive structure.[4] It is reasonable to suppose that the same thing happens in the case of the structure of the self—that a new experience is neutralized or blends into an experiential whole that is not propitious for its development.

In these cases the explanation of the permanence and continuity of the self is very simple. They derive from the permanence of the structure itself. But this does not always happen. There are cases, like that of the soldier mentioned above, in which there takes place a true alteration in the total structure of the self. These facts keep us from resorting to the simplistic form of the category of structure. If we did so, our theory would amount to the verbal substitution of the category of "structure" for that of "substance." Reality obliges us to change our point of view completely, for the immutability of the structural center is untenable.

We have seen that the total structure of the self does not organize the individual experiences but rather organizes the substructures represented by experiential wholes. So then, when the total structure is altered, the substructures that make it up are not reduced to a *tabula rasa*. Instead, these substructures are reorganized into a new pattern. The substructures can keep their inner integrity even though they acquire a different meaning, because they form part of a different structure. Once more an example of visual perception may show what I mean. If to the perceptive structure that we call a cross (Fig. 10)

4. One can change, for example, the size, color, and material of a figure without our ceasing to perceive the same figure. Cf. Köhler, *Gestalt Psychology*, pp. 214-15.

we add two lines (Fig. 11), the cross as such disappears, even though it continues to exist absorbed into the more complicated structure (Fig. 11). That it is still there may be seen by abstracting the two added lines or by considering the fact that one could not come out with Fig. 11 if one took something different than Fig. 10 as his point of departure, such as a triangle, for example.

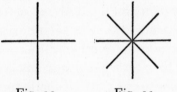

Fig. 10   Fig. 11

This is only an illustrative example.[5] In the structure of the self the process is not so simple. In the first place the first structure does not remain unchanged as it is sub-

5. Fig. 12 is another example of the same kind, while a symphony or a nation could better illustrate the sense of continuity of the self. At the same time, one must not let oneself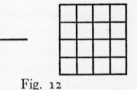

Fig. 12

be deceived by the supposed continuity of some institutions or objects, which may be entirely illusory. How can one talk, for example, of the "same" army if all its leaders, officers, troops, equipment, and objectives have been changed? It is easy to make the mistake of an old Gaucho who thought the world of a knife because it was the "same one" that his grandfather had used, even though he would admit that within the past 30 years he had changed the blade four times and the handle twice.

merged in the one that follows it, for it is a dynamic and not a static structure. Thus it is that the members disappear and at the same time remain, in accordance with the Hegelian concept of *Aufhebung*. Usually what happens is that the substructure present in the foreground is dislodged by another and recedes into the background. In other words the figure becomes ground and the ground figure. So it is with a person, for example, for whom economic interests represent the center of his structure while religious matters are kept in a subordinate position; he goes to church in order to establish commercially useful contacts rather than for religious reasons. A catastrophe—the death of his wife or child or something else of the sort—can change his whole personality. He becomes a religious man. What had been of secondary importance becomes the center about which the structure organizes itself. Economic interests are put to the service of religion, and he hands over his fortune to a monastery. A fundamental change has occurred in his life, but the quantity of elements that remain without having been greatly altered is quite notable. All his intellectual equipment may remain intact, together with his family affections, his artistic tastes, his political ideology, and the greater part of those minor prejudices and beliefs that take part in the constitution of his personality.

The persistence and continuity of our self rest upon former structures. The self is a dynamic structure and is made up of past members and the new ones constantly being added. So to understand a person at a given moment one must know his history, how he has become what he is. This is not the entire story, however, for it omits the creative moment. The self is memory, but memory that looks ahead, is dynamic and creative. For this reason, however radical the change in a person may be, it is a change and not a replacement. The past is still something to be reckoned with, even in cases where we would like to eliminate it altogether. The most radical change in a person—as in a nation—traces his new personality to the past.

B. IMMANENCE AND TRANSCENDENCE OF THE SELF. Another apparent paradox—similar to that of permanence and mutability—which is resolved by the structural conception is that of the immanence and transcendence of the self. For both atomism and substantialism, immanence and transcendence are incompatible. Either the self is equivalent to the totality of experiences—and in this sense is immanent to them—or it is something that transcends the experiences. Atomism holds the first position and substantialism the second.

According to the theory that I am proposing, the self is immanent and transcends experiences at the same time, though admittedly the terms have different meanings from those attributed to them both by atomism and by substantialism. The self is immanent because it is, indeed, equivalent to the totality of experiences; but this totality, in turn, should be interpreted not as the sum or aggregate of the experiences but as a structure that has properties that cannot be found in its parts. According to this interpretation of the concept of totality, the self transcends the experiences and becomes a structural quality, in the sense in which Ehrenfels used this expression. Nevertheless, this is not the transcendence defended by the substantialists when they affirm the existence of a being that supports states or experiences. Mine is a transcendence that not only does not exclude immanence but actually takes it for granted.

Let us look at the problem from another point of view. The relation between the self and its experiences is so intimate that every experience reveals some aspect of the self; what is more, every experience forms part of the self. In this sense, the self seems to be represented in each one of the experiences, to be nothing but them. No experience, however, is able to reveal to us the self in its entirety. Not even the sum of all the experiences can do that. The self is able to transcend its autobiography; hence the possibility of a true repentance, a conversion, a new life. In the first instance the self seems to be immanent; in the second it is seen to be something that transcends its experiences.

The problem is clarified considerably if one turns his attention to those two propositions which Hume, and many others after him, considered to be incompatible: a) that the self is nothing apart from its experiences; b) that the self cannot be reduced to its experiences. I, of course, affirm that both propositions are true. When Hume maintained that the self should be reduced to a bundle of perceptions because it could not exist without them, he let himself be misled by the substantialist prejudice in favor of the so-called independence of the self.

But the self, though not independent of the perceptions, is not reducible to the mere sum of them.

The paradox of the immanence and transcendence of the self, just like the paradox which we examined before, has arisen as a consequence of the way in which substantialists stated the problem of the self, a statement that the atomists accepted without realizing its consequences. The problem, as stated, presupposes a metaphysics and a logic which our conception rejects. First, it conceives of real existence as substance, independent and immutable; and second, it interprets the principles of identity and of noncontradiction in a very rigid way. My concept, on the other hand, gives a very dynamic interpretation to both principles, to the point of seeing in contradiction much of the essence of the real. What is more, I believe that there is nothing independent and immutable. I can hardly believe, therefore, in the independence and immutability of the self, the stuff of which is relationship and the essence of which is creative process.

C. UNITY AND MULTIPLICITY. A variant of the preceding paradoxes is that of unity and multiplicity. When atomism took over the analysis of the self, its unity was destroyed forever and the self was turned into a great mosaic of loose pieces. Each perception became a reality in itself, independent, separable, sharply delimited. With this conception of the elements it proved impossible to rewin the lost unity. Atomists maintained, therefore, the plurality of the self, even though they sighed from time to time for the unity that they themselves had destroyed. When atomists—and men like William James who criticized atomism without being able to free themselves from the source of its confusion—ask what unites the different parts constituting the self, one must simply answer that the self never ceased to constitute a unity. Atomism's difficulties in reaching the unity of the self are merely a consequence of the arbitrary way in which it was dismembered. First they build a wall; then they complain they cannot see beyond the wall.

Substantialism, on the other hand, takes as its point of departure the postulate of unity and relegates multiplicity to accidents. The self is only one, although many different things happen to it.

With the importance that these "happenings" have for us—the self is made up of what it does—the whole statement of the problem collapses; the self is one or multiple according to how one looks at it. It is one if one focuses on the whole; it is multiple if one focuses on the members that constitute it. The self is the unity of the multiplicity of its experiences.

The unity of the self is not like the pseudo unity of a concept that is arrived at by abstraction. Its unity is quite concrete and is arrived at by a process of integration. It is a unity that does not abolish but preserves the differences in the members that make it up. That the self has members does not mean that it can be divided, as one divides a generic concept into the different species that it contains. The self is indivisible, though this does not keep us from distinguishing the different members that constitute it. The self has no existence apart from its members, nor do the members, if separated from the totality of the self, have existence.

D. PSYCHOLOGICAL TYPES. This structural conception of the self opens up new possibilities in the field of typology.

The classifications proposed heretofore have been quite different insofar as the point taken as basis of the classification is concerned, but they resemble each other in one common attitude. Some of them focus upon the predominant value, others upon the biological aspect, still others upon strictly subjective notes, but all these classifications agree in paying attention to what predominates and in ignoring secondary aspects. Gestalt psychology has shown that that which stands out—what Rubin calls the "figure"—acquires different meanings according to its ground. A blue tie, for instance, will have a lighter or darker shade according to whether it has as ground a white shirt or a colored one. If we observe psychological types we shall notice differences that are due not only to the predominant substructure but also to the one that serves as ground. There is no doubt that a person suffering from abulia is different from another person who has normal volition. And he is different not only with regard to will power, which is a mere tautology, but also with regard to emotivity and the total personality. In the same way there are emotivities that exalt and others that depress the intellect, and these, consequently, exercise influence upon the total structure. One has therefore to distinguish each type—emotive, volitive, and intellectual—according to the member that serves as ground.[6]

Applying this principle, we have six basic psychological types instead of the usual three: emotive-intellectual, emotive-volitive, intellectual-volitive, intellectual-emotive, volitive-intellectual, and volitive-emotive. (The first term indicates the predominant substructure, the figure; the other indicates the secondary substructure, the ground.)

The idea proposed here, focusing upon the ground as well as the figure in classifying the psychological types, can be applied equally well to other types of classification. Thus, for example, Spranger distinguishes six types: theoretic, economic, aesthetic, social, political, and religious, in accord with the predominant value. After what has been said, it will be easily seen that in the political type, for example, there can be distinguished five classes, according to the value that serves as ground to the predominant one. And the same thing happens with the other types proposed by Spranger or other thinkers.

Psychologists have always observed that the different types are not fixed, that they change in accordance with age or intense or prolonged experiences. The substantialist conception could never explain these changes because the central nucleus was immutable and resisted the vicissitudes of the different experiences that it went through. The theory that I propose explains both the normal stability of the types and the possibility of change. The sta-

6. This classification in three types was chosen because of its clarity to illustrate the point.

bility of a type derives from the stability of its structure, and change derives from the possibility of the structure's being altered, as was shown in connection with the permanence and mutability of the self.

This theory also gives us a criterion for determining to what psychological type a person belongs. Since the dominant member of the structure tends to impress upon the self the direction which is more adequate for its development, the way to determine to which type a person belongs consists in observing what it is that has meaning for him. In ordinary terms, we want to know what it is that attracts him or repels him and to what he is indifferent. The thing that has meaning for him—whether positive or negative—is that which may be a member in the structure, and it therefore reveals the nature of the structure. What is indifferent may be thrown out, for it reveals no affinity for the predominant structure. In the concrete application of the criterion one must take certain precautions, for other elements may interfere. These may be eliminated only by close observation and comparison with similar cases. So it is, for example, that a man of markedly intellectual structure may show indifference to certain works or activities of an intellectual order. But if this negative attitude is compared with the positive attitude shown toward other intellectual works, it will be discovered that the indifference is due to the special form of the work and not to its intellectual character. In other words, the difficulty will lead us to a more specific determination of the type of his personality.

The thesis proposed here about the psychological types

does not in any sense contradict the conception of the structural unity of the self set forth in our theory of the self as a functional Gestalt. There would be a contradiction only if one interpreted unity in a simplistic sense and considered the members to have a fixed and univocal relation. The unity of the self remains intact, however many distinctions we make between the different substructures, for it is not a static unity based upon homogeneity but a dynamic unity that rests upon the diversity and opposition of the members that make it up.

Index